THIRD EDITION

CHALLENGING CDV

HOW TO AVOID A CRIMINAL DOMESTIC VIOLENCE CONVICTION IN SOUTH CAROLINA

JAMES R. SNELL, JR.

Printed in the United States of America.

ISBN: 978-1-63385-453-6

Designed and published by

Word Association Publishers
205 Fifth Avenue
Tarentum, Pennsylvania 15084

www.wordassociation.com
1.800.827.7903

TABLE OF CONTENTS

DISCLAIMER

This book is intended to provide a general overview of criminal domestic violence prosecution in South Carolina. This book is not intended to provide specific legal advice or instruction on any specific situation. Use of this book does not create an attorney-client relationship between you and the author or the Law Office of James R. Snell, Jr., LLC. This book is based entirely on South Carolina law. The material may be irrelevant or wrong compared to any other state's law. You should always direct any specific questions you have about your case to your own attorney. Sample scenarios in this book refer to "John" and "Mary." These are for the purpose of example only and I am not referring to any specific "John" or "Mary." Any results obtained by the author for one client does not indicate that similar results may be obtained for future clients.

INTRODUCTION

As a practicing criminal defense attorney in South Carolina, I have had the opportunity to advise and represent people arrested for a variety of offenses. These include hundreds of men and woman arrested for domestic violence.

> *My goal is to help people avoid a domestic violence conviction, especially when they have been falsely or unfairly charged. This is accomplished by understanding how to negotiate with professional prosecutors, backed up by the ability to provide an aggressive courtroom defense.*

Many of my domestic violence defense clients have never been arrested before nor have a prior history with the criminal justice system. They arrive in my office scared, confused and unsure how to proceed with their case. My experience has taught me that more people are falsely or unfairly charged with domestic violence in South Carolina than any other crime.

Everyone charged with domestic violence faces the risk of a jail sentence. Many charges come with mandatory jail or prison sentences for those who are unsuccessful with their defense. In addition, there can be steep fines, prohibitions against firearm possession, loss of employment opportunities, complications in family court, mandatory counseling and a criminal record.

I wrote this book to educate not only my clients, but anyone who is facing a domestic violence charge in South Carolina. The material here should be helpful to anyone who has been charged or a loved one who has been accused of a domestic violence offense.

This book may also help you hire the best attorney for your case. While you are reading, you will likely come up with questions about how this material applies to your specific case. I encourage you to keep a list of these questions down and talk about them when you meet with your attorney. The more you know about domestic violence prosecution, the better your chances of success with your own case.

If you would like to consult the Law Office of James R. Snell, Jr., LLC regarding your case, we offer initial consultations at no charge. Appointments are scheduled by calling (803) 636-8826 during normal business hours. My office accepts cases in every part of South Carolina.

You can learn more about my office by visiting our website at *www.cdvlawyer.com*.

INTRODUCTION TO THE 3RD EDITION
AND THE SOUTH CAROLINA DOMESTIC VIOLENCE REFORM ACT

SINCE THE ORIGINAL PUBLICATION OF THIS BOOK IN 2014 there have been important developments in the law. The most significant of which was the Domestic Violence Reform Act passed in 2015. This third edition includes additional information on how cases are prosecuted in General Sessions, as well as on common child abuse charges that are frequently included by law enforcement. Additionally the South Carolina Supreme Court has clarified that those charged with domestic violence may claim self-defense as a bar to prosecution.

South Carolina's domestic violence laws underwent a substantial modification in 2015 with the passage of the Domestic Violence Reform Act. This law affects cases arising after June 4, 2015. As a result, there are several key differences that required updating this book. Key changes include:

- The term "Criminal Domestic Violence" is now being shortened in many instances to just "Domestic Violence." "CDV" may be written as just "DV."

- Tickets are now identified as "DV 3rd Degree," "DV 2nd Degree" and "DV 1st Degree" for most new cases.
- Many first offenses are now prosecuted in General Sessions rather than Magistrate or Municipal Courts.
- Possible jail sentences for first offense cases have increased between three and thirty-six times.

The changes in the law were demanded by special interest groups (many of which have their own agendas) under the guise of protecting South Carolina woman and families. Although the law changes result in drastic penalty increases, there were no additional safeguards put in place to protect citizens against false or unfair arrests.

> *It is now more important than ever for everyone who is facing a domestic violence charge to do everything they can for themselves to ensure that their rights and interests are protected. As a result, I hope that you will find this book to be helpful for you as you work toward achieving success with your own case.*

CHAPTER 1

WHY IS DOMESTIC VIOLENCE DIFFERENT?

In South Carolina, there are many different types of criminal charges. While any arrest that carries a criminal record and a possible jail sentence ought to be taken seriously, there is not another criminal charge that is prosecuted quite like domestic violence.

> *Domestic violence is a very serious criminal offense that makes a variety of conduct illegal. Many people are falsely or unfairly arrested. Thankfully, everyone has the important rights discussed in this book.*

Domestic violence is prosecuted differently than other crimes in South Carolina. Generally speaking, police and the court system as a whole are concerned with a specific incident of criminal conduct. For example, when somebody is arrested and prosecuted for shoplifting, all anybody cares about was, "Did you, or did you not try to steal something?" When somebody is arrested and prosecuted for murder, the question is, "Did you, or did you not kill somebody?" Domestic violence is different because the system and the laws are not just concerned with people who have committed a single incidence of abuse against a spouse or other partner. They are designed to deal with a whole range of personal and family issues. These include issues related to anger management, child abuse, alcohol usage, substance abuse and emotional or physical abuse. These go beyond any single incidence of criminal conduct and encompass behaviors that otherwise wouldn't be considered legal or police matters.

I frequently advise clients that to be arrested, prosecuted and convicted of criminal domestic violence does not require conduct that otherwise would be criminal, domestic or violent.

Why is domestic violence treated differently? South Carolina consistently ranks at the top of the list when it comes to states where women are killed in domestic violence incidents. Our system is designed to ferret out and target those extreme cases. The system will treat everyone and every case as if the people involved could be capable of inflicting serious harm on each other in the future. Because of this, the domestic violence system is designed to deal with people who have the capacity for serious abuse, more so than just isolated incidents or false accusations.

The way that you challenge a domestic violence case can be very different from how you would challenge another type of crime. This is especially true when the main witness the state is a spouse, live-in partner, or someone else with whom the defendant has a close relationship. For example, when you go to court in a regular criminal case, you can try to make the state's witness look bad to cast doubt on the charge against you. But it is hard to use those same heavy-handed tactics when it is someone you love or care for.

Many defendants and their families are immediately frustrated when they discover how domestic violence is different from other types of charges. While there is a reason for how the police and court system respond to these situations, it isn't in any sort of intuitive or common-sense way. The most important thing that anyone who is dealing with a domestic violence case from any perspective (defendant, family member or even defense attorney) can do is to appreciate these differences at the onset of the case. In order to be successful with a domestic violence case, you have to understand these differences and incorporate them into a defense strategy.

It is my hope that by reading this book, you and your family will be better prepared to resolve your pending domestic violence case. I encourage you to learn as much about the law as possible, and then to use that information to help you select the best attorney for your case so that the two of you can plan the most effective strategy for a successful outcome.

CHAPTER 2

WHAT IS CRIMINAL DOMESTIC VIOLENCE IN SOUTH CAROLINA?

Domestic violence is a criminal offense. All charges are brought by the state, not by a private individual. It can either be a misdemeanor or a felony. To be arrested for domestic violence, the police must believe that there was an illegal physical act, an attempted illegal act, or some type of language or other action that made someone believe an illegal act was about to happen. You are charged with criminal domestic violence if your ticket or arrest warrant refers to any "CDV" or "DV" offense.

Anyone can be arrested for criminal domestic violence. Although the law was written mostly to help women trapped in abusive relationships, a significant number of women are now being arrested and prosecuted. People of any age can also be arrested. I represented a teenager in high school charged with domestic violence. At the other extreme, I represented a woman in her 80s who was arrested after getting into a physical argument with her husband of nearly 60 years.

For an offense to be criminal domestic violence, it is necessary that the person arrested, called the defendant, and the person who is alleged to be the victim have some type of special relationship. This relationship is called household member. To be a household member, the defendant and alleged victim must either be spouses, divorced, have children in common, or are currently cohabitating or have cohabitated in the past. There can be some special issues in determining whether or not a household member status exists, and they are an often, overlooked area of defense for a criminal domestic violence charge.

No matter what occurred, if there is no household member status there can be no violation of the domestic violence law. There are many different strategies that I have employed to defeat criminal domestic violence allegations based on the state's inability to prove a household member relationship.

> *The household member requirement must be proven in court beyond a reasonable doubt, exactly like the illegal act at issue. If the court has reasonable doubt about the relationship between you and the alleged victim, the court must find you not guilty of domestic violence.*

Although the official criminal domestic violence statute in South Carolina uses the term "physical harm or injury" to define what acts constitute domestic violence, this phrase has been interpreted by our courts to encompass just about any type of non-consensual contact, including contact that otherwise would be described as rude or unwanted. Because of how the law is interpreted, law enforcement and the courts have extremely broad discretion in determining whether something constitutes illegal domestic violence.

Recent changes in the law have also allowed for DV arrests to occur with same-sex couples. If this applies to your situation, the same law and court procedures will apply in your case as in any other.

EXAMPLES OF CRIMINAL DOMESTIC VIOLENCE

- A wife punches her husband in the face.
- An angry man intentionally wrecks his car with his wife inside.
- A husband pushes his wife on the couch.
- A woman angrily throws an object at her child's father.
- A child's father threatens the mother with a knife.
- A drunken woman throws a beer can at her husband (and misses).

EXAMPLES THAT ARE NOT CRIMINAL DOMESTIC VIOLENCE

- A husband accidently knocks his wife down a flight of stairs.
- A boyfriend who only sleeps over occasionally kicks his girlfriend.
- A drunken woman slaps her date on their first time out.
- A man and woman consensually engage in rough intimate activity.
- A woman hits her child's father in self-defense.
- A man threatens a woman he just met at a bar.

Incidents involving non household members may instead be prosecuted under South Carolina's Assault and Battery laws. In addition, when someone is charged with domestic violence the court is authorized to instead find them guilty of Assault and Battery if it isn't satisfied of the household member relationship. The Assault and Battery law is reviewed further in Chapter 25.

CHAPTER 3

TYPES OF DOMESTIC VIOLENCE CHARGES "IS MY CASE A MISDEMEANOR OR A FELONY?"

THERE ARE FOUR DIFFERENT TYPES OF DOMESTIC VIOLENCE charges in South Carolina. If your domestic violence case is referred to any Magistrate Court or Municipal (City) Court, then it is a misdemeanor. DV 3rd Degree and DV 2nd Degree charges are misdemeanors. DV 1st Degree and DVHAN are felonies.

One way you can tell if the court is Magistrate or Municipal is to check to see if it handles evictions. If so, then it is a Magistrate Court. The only types of cases Municipal Courts are allowed to hear are criminal and traffic offenses.

> *Everyone charged with a DV 3rd Degree violation on a traffic ticket has been charged with a misdemeanor. You can also be certain that your case is a misdemeanor if your court date is assigned to "Domestic Violence Court," Magistrate Court or Municipal Court.*

Following is a summary of the four different domestic violence charges.

DV 3rd Degree:	Misdemeanor tried in Magistrate or City Court. Punishable by up to 90 days in jail.
DV 2nd Degree:	Misdemeanor tried in General Sessions. Punishable by up to three years in the South Carolina Department of Corrections.
DV 1st Degree:	Felony tried in General Sessions. Punishable by up to ten years in the South Carolina Department of Corrections.
DVHAN:	(*Domestic Violence of a High Aggravated Nature*) Felony tried in General Sessions. Punishable by up to twenty years in prison.

CHAPTER 4

CDV PENALTIES *OR* "AM I GOING TO GO TO JAIL?"

THE MOST COMMON CONCERN PEOPLE HAVE AFTER BEING arrested for domestic violence is whether they will go to jail. All domestic violence cases present some possibility of a jail sentence, and no lawyer can ever promise you 100% that you will not go to jail. However, after having represented hundreds of domestic violence defendants throughout South Carolina I can usually identify which cases present a higher risk of an actual jail sentence.

> *All Domestic Violence Offenses Carry a Possible Jail Sentence, Even for those Arrested for False or Unfair Allegations.*

The most common domestic violence offense is DV 3rd Degree. It carries a sentence of up to 90 days in jail for those who either plead guilty or plead no contest, or who are found guilty after either a judge or jury trial. Most defendants who are convicted of DV 3rd are not at much risk of going to jail as long as they do not have a serious prior criminal record and are willing to pay a fine or do mandatory counselling. But there are some circumstances that will make it more likely that someone will face jail time:

- Allegations that the alleged victim was choked.
- Evidence that the alleged victim was injured, such as a busted lip or black eye.
- Photographs showing blood.
- If the defendant has a prior criminal history, especially of felonies, assaults, or prior domestic violence offenses.
- When the defendant is also alleged to have been rude to or resisted law enforcement.
- Domestic violence cases where the defendant was also arrested for another offense like drug possession, child endangerment or a weapons violation.
- When the alleged victim later tells the victim's advocate or the court that the defendant threatened them if they came to court or didn't change their story.

If one of these applies to your case, it is even more important that you contact an attorney with experience in difficult domestic violence cases. There are strategies that can help you in your case, including voluntarily enrolling in counselling before you go to court, that can help you minimize the risk of going to jail and may even give you a realistic chance of successfully negotiating a resolution with the prosecutor.

Besides jail, there are other penalties that you can face if convicted of any domestic violence crime:

- High fines (over $5,000 for a DV 3rd Degree, more for other charges).
- Publicly available criminal record.

- Loss of a professional license or the ability to pass employment screenings.
- Restrictions against purchasing or possessing a firearm.
- Loss of a concealed weapons permit (CWP).
- Potential deportation.
- Some foreign countries will not allow you to enter with either a pending domestic violence case or once you have been convicted of one. (I have a consultant available who can help my clients gain entrance into Canada while their case is pending)
- Family Court rulings that could impact how property is divided during divorce, whether alimony is paid or how time with children is allotted.
- Immediate termination or exclusion from military or law enforcement jobs.

IMMIGRATION CONSEQUENCES

Anyone who is not a full citizen of the United States should be especially concerned about any criminal domestic violence charge. Federal law mandates that domestic violence charges be considered when a renewing residency or citizenship application. Convictions for domestic violence (even DV 3rd Degree) may result in a non-citizen being deported from the United States. Tell your defense attorney during your first meeting if you are not an American citizen. In my practice, I arrange for a consultation with an immigration attorney on behalf of all my non-citizen CDV defense clients.

CHAPTER 5

BURDEN OF PROOF "HOW MUCH EVIDENCE DO THE POLICE NEED?"

THE LAW REQUIRES ONLY THAT THERE IS PROBABLE CAUSE TO support the arrest. Even though all domestic violence cases are very serious, there is usually little or no investigation by the police before they decide to make an arrest. Probable cause is significantly less than the level of proof needed to convict those who fight their case in court.

> *Police need probable cause to arrest you for any domestic violence charge. A court needs proof beyond a reasonable doubt to convict you. This is a much higher standard.*

An important concept is that the law generally considers the significance of evidence to be in the "eye of the beholder." A domestic violence case doesn't require any one specific type of evidence. It can all be based on just a single eyewitness account. If that one witness is believable enough, their testimony could be enough to support a domestic violence arrest or conviction. The following example illustrates this point:

Mary and John have been married for several years. Mary has a history of alcohol abuse. Police have been called to their house before but have always left without arresting anyone. This time, though, Mary was so drunk and angry that she told the police that John had pulled her hair. When the police questioned John, he denied touching Mary at all and told the police that she was lying. Although no one else was home, there were no visible injuries to Mary and the police could tell that John had not been drinking. Still, they believed that Mary was so upset that she was likely telling the truth. John was arrested for DV 3rd Degree.

In that example, the police could legally find probable cause just based on Mary's drunken assertion that her hair had been pulled, even with John denying touching her at all. Mary's story was enough to have John arrested, though it was not supported by any other evidence.

Here is another example where it worked out better for John:

Mary and John are not married but have two children in common. Mary has been dating Steve for the last several weeks. Steve and John have known each other since high school and do not get along. Mary is now angry with John because he is late with his child support. When John shows up to pick up the children for his weekend, Mary is waiting for him on the front porch. She yells at him and tells him that he is never going to see the children again and that she is in love with Steve. When John insists on picking up the children, Mary calls 9-1-1 and reports that John has hit her. Mary then calls Steve to come over. When the police arrive, they talk to Steve, who says that he saw the whole thing and that John hit Mary. Mary also has a bruise on her arm that she says John caused. John denies hitting Mary. This time, even though there is another witness (Steve) and bruises on Mary's arm, the police don't believe

> *Mary. They are not sure what happened, but think it is more likely that John didn't do anything wrong. The police do not arrest anyone and, instead, advise John to go to Family Court to get help with his visitation issue.*

Probable cause for a domestic violence arrest simply means that it more likely happened than not. If there is a 51% chance it happened and a 49% chance it didn't happen, that's enough to justify an arrest. You can take that one step further. For example, say two people are arguing and the police respond; all the police have to be convinced of is that there's a 51% chance that criminal domestic violence occurred and a 51% chance that John, rather than Mary, committed it. At that point, John's the one who gets arrested. Legally, John may be arrested even when everyone agrees that the law might not have been broken or that it may have been broken by Mary instead.

When any domestic violence case goes to court for a trial, the court is not allowed to find the defendant guilty if all the evidence shows is that there was probable cause. The law requires that the police or prosecutor submit enough evidence to prove that the defendant is guilty beyond a reasonable doubt. If at the end of a trial the jury only thinks that the defendant is most likely guilty, then they will be instructed that they have no choice but to find the defendant not guilty.

Reasonable doubt is the highest level of legal proof required in our court system. It has been defined by the South Carolina Supreme Court as "the kind of doubt that would cause a reasonable person to hesitate to act." By that they mean that if a jurors hesitates about whether they should find a defendant guilty, that hesitation is the type of doubt that should result in a not guilty verdict.

Under our system, there should be many circumstances where the police can legally make an arrest (with the probable cause standard), but the defendant should be found not guilty if they take their case to trial (due to the high reasonable doubt standard). One of the most important jobs for a defense attorney is to show the court during trial how the reasonable doubt that exists requires that the defendant be found not guilty.

CHAPTER 6

NO DROP POLICY "CAN'T THIS JUST GO AWAY?"

A GENERAL RULE EXISTS CALLED THE "NO DROP POLICY" THAT applies to all levels of criminal domestic violence. This rule says that police or prosecutors are not allowed to drop a domestic violence case before it goes to court. Many people think that their case will be dismissed if their partner just asks. This is not how cases are resolved in South Carolina.

> *The "no drop policy" keeps the police from dismissing your case just because someone asks them. It does not keep you from being found not-guilty at trial, winning a legal dismissal, plea bargaining or going into pre-trial intervention.*

The "no drop policy" began several years ago due to an order from the South Carolina attorney general's office. That office was sending prosecutors to different parts of South Carolina and re-opening domestic violence cases that the police had dismissed. This policy is still in effect today.

Mary immediately felt bad that John was being arrested. She cried as she watched the police handcuff him and take him to jail. The next day, she went to the police department and delivered a letter explaining how if John was prosecuted for domestic violence, he might lose his job and then her family would be destitute. Even though the police officer who arrested John was sorry about her situation, the no drop policy prohibited him from dismissing the case.

The reason for this policy is that when someone is a true victim of domestic violence, he or she may not want to see their partner prosecuted. There is also concern that a defendants might threaten or intimidate their partner into dropping the charges. Because of this, a blanket rule is applied in all cases that prevent domestic violence cases from being disposed of outside of court.

But it is very important to note that the no drop policy does not keep the case from being resolved in other ways. It does not stop a court from finding a defendant not guilty. It does not prevent people from getting referred to PTI. It does not prevent plea bargains such as when a DVHAN is reduced down to a misdemeanor with no jail time. It means that all cases have to be resolved in court through some type of agreement or negotiation that occurs at the courthouse.

CHAPTER 7

MIRANDA ADVISEMENTS "WHAT IF THE POLICE DID NOT READ ME MY RIGHTS?"

Everyone who has ever watched a police show on TV is familiar with Miranda advisements given to people while they are being arrested. Miranda is usually provided similar to the following:

> *You have a right to remain silent. Anything you say can and may be used against you. You have a right to an attorney and to have that attorney present with you during questioning. If you cannot afford an attorney, one will be provided to you. If you decide to answer questions, you have a right to stop at any time.*

The legal significance of Miranda advisements has to do with whether answers that you gave the police to questions they asked you after you were in custody can be repeated in court and used against you.

If the police did not advise you of your Miranda rights, this may prevent the police from being able to repeat in court certain statements that you made. It does not mean that your case will automatically be thrown out, especially if there is other evidence that could be used against you. Examples of other types of evidence would be statements you made before you were in custody, statements made by other people against you or photographs taken by the police.

In South Carolina, there is only one crime in which the police must give Miranda rights in order to have a valid arrest. That crime is drunk driving. Although Miranda has to be given to every defendant in order to have answers to questions repeated in court, the law does not require that Miranda be given if the police can make their case using other evidence.

The following example illustrates this point:

> *The police have responded to an argument between John and Mary. The police begin by taking Mary outside and talking to her on the driveway. John is kept inside the house. Neither one has been placed under arrest and both would have been free to leave anytime they wanted. After the police questioned them for a few minutes, they decided that John was guilty of DV 3rd Degree. John was then told that he was under arrest. At this time, the police did not read him his Miranda rights. The police continued to ask him questions, including how many times he hit Mary. John admitted to them then that he had hit Mary at least five or six times.*

In the example, John is still legally arrested even without having been given his Miranda rights. The statements that he made about having hit Mary at least five or six times will not be allowed as evidence against him at a trial. If John had been given his Miranda rights, then everything he said could have been used against him.

MIRANDA TIPS

- If the police did not read you your Miranda rights, your case will not automatically be thrown out.
- If you chose to remain silent and not answer police questions, then it does not matter if they did or did not read you your rights.
- If you say that the police did not read you your Miranda rights and the police say they did, then the court has to decide who is telling the truth.
- People who were not arrested (such as witnesses) do not have Miranda rights read to them.

CHAPTER 8

RIGHT TO REMAIN SILENT

Everyone in South Carolina has a right to remain silent when questioned by the police. The best advice I have for anyone who is being investigated by law enforcement is to not say anything or answer any questions until you have consulted with an attorney.

> *We always recommend that anyone who is being investigated by the police for any crime should not agree to meet with the police or answer any questions until you have first talked with a lawyer.*

The right to remain silent also applies in all court proceedings. The police, prosecutor or judge can never make anyone who has been arrested answer questions or talk in or out of court. Defendants exercise this right at a trial by choosing not to testify. If you do decide to testify, the prosecutor is then allowed to ask you questions. This is called cross examination. Even if you choose to remain silent, your lawyer is still allowed to talk and can address the judge or jury at appropriate times, cross examine all of the prosecution witnesses and question any witnesses who are going to testify in your favor.

If you remain silent at trial, the judge will instruct the jury that they are not allowed to consider your silence when deciding your case. They will be instructed that they are not even allowed to talk about the fact that you chose not to testify.

The only times during the court process that you do not have the right to remain silent is if you decide to plead guilty (because you have to let the court know that you are pleading guilty) or if you have already testified and then it is the prosecutor's turn to ask you questions.

One important reason people choose not to testify at trial is if they have a prior criminal record that the prosecutor could use against them in court. If you have certain types of criminal convictions that are no more than ten years old, they may be brought up if you do testify. Your lawyer can talk to you about your rights in court and can give you advice as to the decision you should make. It is, however, always your choice whether or not you testify.

The right to remain silent is an absolute right only of the defendant. Other witnesses may be required to answer questions and may be held in contempt of court if they refuse to answer them.

CHAPTER 9

BOND COURT

Bond Court is a type of hearing presided over by a Magistrate Court judge. Every county has its own Bond Court, as well as some cities. The purpose of Bond Court is to decide under what conditions a defendant may be allowed to leave before the assigned court date. Only cases in which the defendant was arrested and taken to jail have to go to Bond Court. Bond hearings are usually held either the same day or the day after an arrest. You can find out the location and time of the bond hearing by contacting the jail where the defendant was taken.

> *Bond is the "deal" you make with the government to allow you out of jail while your case is pending. It can consist of money paid or pledged to the court, or other restrictions such as no contact with the alleged victim.*

Defendants have a right to be represented by an attorney in Bond Court. Because the hearings are held so soon after arrest, it is important that if you want an attorney to be present that you contact one immediately after the arrest. At the bond hearing, the judge will consider the defendant's risk to the community as well as their risk of flight. Defendants should avoid making any statement on the facts of their case in Bond Court, as these may be used against them later. There is typically no opportunity for friends or family to interact with the defendant in Bond Court or to participate in the hearing. If you plan on appearing, be sure to listen carefully as official charges are announced and other instructions may be given by the judge. Bond hearings are usually very brief, even on serious charges.

At the conclusion of the hearing, the judge will announce the decision. The judge may set a personal recognize (PR) bond. In a PR bond, the defendant promises to appear in court and is released on his word. If the defendant fails to appear, he can be fined by the court or face an absentee trial and even additional criminal charges. In other cases, a judge may order cash or a security bond. In this type of bond, the defendant or someone on the defendant's behalf must post money with the Bond Court as a condition of the defendant's release. If the defendant fails to appear in court or violates other terms of his or her bond, the money may be forfeited. Often, a bail bondsman is hired to post the bond on a defendant's behalf. A bail bondsman will handle all of the paperwork with the Bond Court. Their fee is usually a percentage of the bond amount. The standard fee is 10%, but this may vary depending on location and the exact circumstances of the case. The bondsman's fee is not considered refundable, even if the defendant appears in court. Once bond is posted, it is usually several hours before the defendant will be released from jail.

In addition to setting a bond amount, the Bond Court also may set other conditions on the defendant's release. These may include no contact with the alleged victim or electronic monitoring. Defendants from out of state should be aware that it is a standard bond condition that they may not leave South Carolina while they are awaiting trial. If a defendant violates any of these terms, bond may be revoked even if the defendant hasn't missed any court dates.

If bond is not set by the Bond Court for any reason or if a prohibitively high bond is set, the defendant may petition the court of General Sessions for a bond setting or bond reduction hearing. It is important to have your attorney request this type of hearing. Once requested, it may take several weeks to have a hearing scheduled.

TIPS FOR BOND COURT SUCCESS

- Immediately after the arrest, find out the time and place of the Bond Court. Verify any information the police gave you about the schedule by calling the court directly.
- If you plan on attending Bond Court, arrive at least 15 minutes early to ensure that you have time to be screened by security. Dress for court. This means no shorts or tank tops. Turn your phone off or better yet, leave it in your car.
- If it is a felony level charge, consider hiring a lawyer for the Bond Court appearance. A lawyer may be able to help lower the bond amount set by the court and can answer many of your questions about the procedure.
- Keep track of all important information given by the judge, including the next court date and any special conditions on release.

CHAPTER 10

NO CONTACT BOND RESTRICTIONS "WHAT DO YOU MEAN I CAN'T GO HOME?"

A STANDARD CONDITION ON DOMESTIC VIOLENCE BONDS throughout South Carolina is the no contact restriction. In many areas, nearly all domestic violence defendants have bond restrictions put in place. Other counties are different. Whether or not the Bond Court placed a bond restriction on your case has no bearing on how serious you should be taking your case.

Bond restrictions give domestic violence defendants more problems than anything else while their case is pending. The no contact order is usually defined as don't call, don't write, don't email, don't text, don't Facebook, no smoke signals, don't wave, don't stand behind them in line at the supermarket, don't go to their house. Just stay completely away and have absolutely no contact. Any violation of the no contact order can result in either the bond being completely revoked, meaning a return to jail with no chance of leaving until their case is over, or being held in contempt of court, with a punishment of up to 30 days for each instance of violation.

For example, four text messages between a defendant and an alleged victim could result in up to 120 days in jail. After that time is served and the defendant is released, the no contact order is still in place and the domestic violence is still pending. The no contact restriction applies to any contact that the defendant has with the alleged victim, even if the alleged victim initiates the contact or agrees to the contact. Let me give an example:

> *John and Mary have an argument and John is arrested for domestic violence. Mary is immediately apologetic, saying that she is sorry that this happened, that there is no need for him to be arrested and that she has no intention on breaking off the relationship and, in fact, wants to get back with him as soon as possible. After John gets out of jail, Mary finds out he's staying at his mother's house. After trying to reach John by telephone, Mary drives to John's mother's house. She knocks on the door and is let inside by John's mother. Mary comes inside the living room where John is sitting watching TV. John does not immediately get up and leave the house, but instead listens to Mary talk about their children's upcoming school schedule and about how they will pay the household expenses. Later, the police learn about this meeting from John's mother, who didn't know her son had done anything wrong. The police notify the judge, who issues an order for John to appear in court. John does and is immediately sentenced to thirty days in jail. He is not allowed to post bond to get out.*

The no contact order can be violated even when contact was initiated by the alleged victim or consensual between the parties. This is important because no contact bond restrictions should be considered unilateral. They don't apply to the alleged victim. If the defendant was told in bond court to have no contact with the alleged victim, even if the alleged victim is the one who calls, emails, or comes to the house and knocks on the door, the defendant violates the bond if he answers the phone, replies to an email or opens the door. The person who initiates the contact doesn't get in any trouble because there are no court restrictions against them. No contact bond restrictions can be modified, but a court order is needed and that almost always requires a hearing.

Many people believe that if the alleged victim requests that the bond restriction goes away, then the bond restriction goes away. Some people may try to submit a letter or notarized statement to the court thinking that is all that is necessary. That is not true. Because a very high percentage of my domestic violence cases have no contact bond restrictions, I have developed a specific system and checklist to help my clients obtain relief as quickly as possible.

My system involves scheduling a meeting with the alleged victim to make sure that they are on board with the bond being modified. I like to have a chance to verify firsthand what their position will be, so it does not come as a surprise to us later in court. If we learn they do not want the restrictions modified (for any reason), the court will not lift the restrictions. This is true no matter how inconvenient the restrictions are for my client.

If the alleged victim is on board, the next step is to have them submit a statement to the court acknowledging their consent of the bond modification. Then, we work with the court to have a hearing scheduled. I like to have the case discovery materials before going into a hearing. Our client and the alleged victim both need to be at this hearing. Usually, the police officer, prosecutor or victim's advocate will talk to the alleged victim in private to make sure that he wasn't pressured by the defendant. The judge will question the alleged victim to make sure he is really in agreement.

The alleged victim may be asked if you have violated the no contact order. If the court learns you have, not only may the judge refuse to modify your bond but you could face an immediate contempt hearing as well.

After the judge has the chance to consider a request for the no contact order at the hearing, the judge's decision is usually written down in the court's file. Your lawyer may choose to follow up with the judge by submitting a proposed order. Bond restrictions are designed to remain in place as long as the case is open. CDV cases that are being challenged or going to PTI may stay open for months. So, it is a good idea to have bond restrictions lifted or at least modified if the defendant and the alleged victim are going to want to continue their relationship, have children or a enter into joint business interests.

PRACTICAL TIPS ABOUT BOND RESTRICTIONS

- If a CDV defendant is being harassed by the alleged victim, the defendant has a right to file for a restraining order in Magistrate Court. If the defendant and alleged victim are married or have children together, they can ask for a restraining order in Family Court. If the alleged victim continues to harass the defendant after a restraining order is put in place, it is the victim who goes to jail. Always discuss the idea of getting a restraining order with a CDV defense attorney first.

- Do not think you can get away violating a no contact bond restriction. Police actively look for violators and if you are caught, the penalty can be swiftly – and severely – imposed.

- Criminal Court no contact orders and Family Court restraining orders are two separate things. Just because one judge says you can have contact does not automatically change another judge's order.

- Although you can ask the court to modify bond on any domestic violence charge, it may take a long time to have your request heard if your case is pending in General Sessions.

CHAPTER 11

HIRING A DEFENSE ATTORNEY

It is my hope that the material in this book will be helpful for anyone who has been arrested for any domestic violence crime. The best two pieces of advice I have for anyone who has been arrested is to learn as much as you can about the law and court procedures and to hire a lawyer who will give you the level of representation that you deserve. While this book can give you a general overview of domestic violence law, I have included the following questions that you should ask any lawyer you are considering hiring for your case. You may ask these questions directly, or listen for the lawyer to talk about them as part of their initial meeting with you:

1. In what ways are domestic violence cases treated differently by the prosecutor or the court from other criminal cases?
2. Do you think that enrolling in a counseling program might help my case? Why or why not?
3. What is the exact process you employ to help get no contact bond restrictions lifted?
4. Have you actually tried a domestic violence case to verdict before a jury?
5. Have you appealed a criminal conviction for a client?

6. Do you have prepared jury charges or instructions specific for domestic violence cases?
7. How often do you accompany your clients to Family Court hearings when an order of protection has been requested?
8. How much will you charge to take my case? How did you come up with that amount?
9. What is your office's client communication policy? How frequently are calls returned?
10. Are you a member of the South Carolina Association of Criminal Defense Lawyers? (This is the most important group to which any criminal defense attorney in South Carolina can belong.)

> *Legally, no attorney can claim to be an expert or specialist in the area of domestic violence defense. It is unethical for an attorney to ever make you any promise or guarantee regarding how your case will turn out.*

LEGAL FEES

My office normally charges a flat rate for defending a domestic violence case. The fee is set during the initial consultation and covers all of the services that will be provided to the client by my office during their case. We do not charge extra for travel, mileage, court appearances or trial.

You may find a significant range of fees charged by other lawyers. Some lawyers try to charge the lowest prices in town. Other lawyers try to charge the highest prices in town. There is not always a relationship between the fee charged by a lawyer and the quality of the services that they will provide.

I am not the least expensive defense attorney, but at the same time I do not try to charge the highest prices either. The fee set is designed to be fair both to my client and to me after taking into account the specific nature of the case. Because my fee is determined after I have had a chance to learn about the client's case and about their specific objectives, it is usually impossible to quote a fair fee over the telephone. Any lawyer you hire should be able to easily explain the fees you will be responsible for after you meet with. Fee and representation agreements should also be put in writing.

CHAPTER 12

BENCH TRIAL VS. JURY TRIAL "DOES MY CASE HAVE TO GO TO A JURY?"

PERSONS ARRESTED FOR DV 3RD DEGREE, THEY WILL USUALLY receive a traffic ticket with a court date on it or will be given a court date in Bond Court. This date may be just a couple of weeks after the arrest was made. Many people want to know what's going to happen at that court date. For most defendants, the answer is nothing good.

> *DV 3rd Degree charges are usually given on a traffic ticket. You do not automatically get a jury trial on a DV 3rd Degree case; you must ask for it in advance. By default, your case is decided by a single judge.*

If you go to court on the first date given to you for a DV 3rd Degree, typically you will find a judge on the bench who is expecting to either take a guilty plea or immediately go to trial. Defendants who show up at this date expect to forego most of their important legal rights. These rights could potentially help you be found not guilty or favorably negotiate your case. There is usually no advantage for anyone to give up these rights, so I strongly recommend that anyone charged with domestic violence talk to a lawyer before their first court date. Consulting with a lawyer will give you access to all available defense strategies that can help avoid a conviction.

What rights are given up by just going to the first court date? Because the cases are scheduled so quickly after the arrest, there's no time for a process called pre-trial discovery. A defendant has the right to get copies of witness statements, video or audio recorded interviews, photographs, police reports and other documents that may serve as the basis for the arrest. These records are very important to defendants wishing to challenge their case. The right to discovery is provided by the South Carolina Rules of Criminal Procedure as well as legal opinions from both the South Carolina Supreme Court and the United States Supreme Court.

> *There are six jurors who serve in Magistrate or Municipal court cases. General Sessions juries have twelve jurors.*

Another important right is the right to a trial by jury. A judge in a bench trial is going to be concerned with whether the law was violated and, if violated, that was there unwanted physical contact, attempted contact or threat of contact. A jury will have six people who must unanimously decide beyond a reasonable doubt that the defendant is guilty of domestic violence. Any six jurors will have more life experience than any single judge. They will know that not every argument or accusation should result in someone being arrested or convicted in court. There is a reason why the right to a trial by jury is one of those most fundamental in our legal system, and it is because of this that it offers the best protection against a false or unfair criminal conviction.

The technical reading of domestic violence law is, frankly, not favorable to a defendant. A judge may feel like they are required to convict somebody because that person threw a pillow or poured a bowl of cereal on someone's head (I have defended against those both those allegations in several different cases). A jury that understands the same facts may be highly unlikely to find that there was domestic violence because they simply can't believe that's what the law should do and they won't be able, in good conscience, to brand somebody a criminal for that type of action. In a bench trial, even if you have a judge who is as fair and as good as any single juror can be for a defendant, a conviction requires only one person to be convinced beyond a reasonable doubt (the judge) and not six people (the jury panel). At the end of a trial if a single juror is not convinced beyond a reasonable doubt, then the defendant will not be convicted.

SHOULDN'T I CHECK FIRST TO SEE IF THE JUDGE THINKS I NEED A JURY?

I have been asked by several people with cases pending if they should see what the judge thinks they should do about their case. Their idea is to try to save money on legal fees by talking to the judge at their first court date.

> *No one else except for the criminal defense attorney who is working for you is allowed to give you legal or strategy advice about your case. This includes the police, prosecutor, victim's advocate, court staff or even the judge. While anyone of them may tell you that you have a right to a trial or even a right to a jury trial, none of them is allowed to give you advice about what decision you should make.*

When you report to your first court date, your first opportunity to speak to the judge is likely going to be in the context of your trial. The law does not allow judges to talk to people about pending cases without the other side being there (and for a DV 3rd Degree case, the other side is the police officer who arrested you or the prosecutor). This law also prevents judges from taking your phone calls. Once the judge hears your case, he might immediately find you guilty. You don't then get to say, "Hold on. I'd like a jury now" or "I'd like to get a lawyer." In most circumstances, a judge finding you guilty after the bench trial is the final decision in the case. People take a lot of risk by attempting to represent themselves at the initial court date.

In South Carolina, the court is not legally allowed to conduct a hearing before the start of a domestic violence trial to determine if there is enough evidence to allow the case to be prosecuted. Although such a hearing exists for General Sessions cases (called the preliminary hearing), it does not apply to DV 3rd Degree cases. The South Carolina Supreme Court made this very clear in a 2009 legal decision involving a criminal domestic violence case from Rock Hill. Decisions of the Supreme Court apply to every city or county in the state. This rule prevents the judge from dismissing your case based on insufficient evidence unless they are conducting an actual trial and the state has presented all of its evidence.

THE SOLUTION

After representing hundreds of people charged with all levels of domestic violence around South Carolina, I have developed a system and a checklist to help give my clients the best possibility of successfully resolving their case.

Although I remain flexible to adapt for special cases, most of the time I do the following within the first 24 hours of being hired for any domestic violence case:

- Draft and file a formal jury trial request with the court.
- Draft and file initial discovery motions (usually titled Brady and Rule 5).
- Send a letter of representation to the prosecutor or arresting police officer. Include copies of the legal motions and jury trial request.
- Begin work on a modification of any applicable "no contact" bond restriction.

Once these initial filings are made, my client does not have to go to the first court date and risk appearing in front of the judge alone. This procedure is approved by the South Carolina Supreme Court and is allowed in every court in South Carolina. It is also allowed by every bail bondsman in the state.

The next court event is usually a pre-trial conference held weeks or even a few months later. By the time of this conference, I like to have the discovery documents from the prosecutor so I know the case from their side as well as from my client's. I am able to go to the pre-trial conference prepared to discuss the case with the prosecutor without any pressure of an immediate trial. This puts us in the best position to negotiate the most favorable resolution to the case possible. If we are able to work the case out at this conference by some type of plea bargain or pre-trial intervention, then the case does not have to go in front a jury for trial.

In addition to the foregoing, I also consider the following:

- Referring my client to voluntarily participate in alcohol, drug, or domestic abuse counseling.
- Retaining a private investigator to conduct a defense-oriented investigation into the facts and circumstances of the arrest (we typically always do this for DV 2nd Degree and higher charges).
- Request other police reports involving the alleged victim or other witnesses to the case through the use of the Freedom of Information Act (FOIA).

CHAPTER 13

THE DISCOVERY PROCESS

Discovery refers to the process by which a criminal defendant may access police reports, witness statements, photographs, and other materials before trial. This chapter reviews the process of discovery in a typical domestic violence case. While discovery is something that your lawyer will typically handle, it's helpful for you to have a general understanding of the process.

DISCOVERY MOTIONS

The most common way discovery is obtained in South Carolina domestic violence cases is by the filing of formal discovery motions with the court. This is typically in the form of a "Rule 5" and "Brady" motion. These motions will be written and prepared in your lawyer's office.

"Rule 5" motions are based on Rule 5 of the South Carolina Rules of Criminal Procedure. This rule outlines a specific list of materials that should be turned over upon request. This includes statements of the defendant, police reports, witness statements, the defendant's prior criminal history, and reports of scientific tests.

"Brady" refers to discovery requests made pursuant to a 1963 United States Supreme Court case called Brady vs Maryland. Because this case was decided by the United States Supreme Court, it applies to every court in the country, including all South Carolina criminal and domestic violence courts. Generally, the Brady case requires the prosecution to turn over to the defense any evidence that could clear the defendant of the charge.

After these motions are prepared, they will be filed with the court. This simply means that they are given to a court clerk. This can be done in-person or by mail. They will then be served on the police officer or prosecutor for the case. The filing and service of the motion will also be handled by your lawyer's office.

It typically takes several weeks or months in order for the defense to be provided with the discovery materials. In practice (the real world), there is no automatic time-frame by which discovery materials must be provided by. When necessary, the judge can give a deadline that the materials must be made available by. If discovery materials are not provided by a deadline assigned by the judge, or by a trial date (not simply a pretrial date), the judge can then either continue the case or can dismiss it.

Discovery materials may be provided in paper form (such as copies of reports or handwritten statements), or in electronic form (such as PDF files, photographs, and videos). In some areas discovery documents will be mailed to your lawyer's office. In other areas they are available from a computer service made available to your lawyer. And in other areas it may be normal for discovery to be provided at a pretrial conference (not necessarily the first one). Your lawyer can advise you on what the normal practice is you may expect in your case.

POLICE REPORTS ARE NOT EVIDENCE

A police report will be prepared by the police officer(s) who respond to a domestic violence call, or who make an arrest. The report itself is not considered evidence by the court. If your domestic violence case went to trial, the jury would not normally be allowed to read or even look at the police report. The report is simply the police officer's notes, where the officer would record the most important information. It's also important to consider what information the police report doesn't include. In court a defense attorney can argue inferences favorable to the defense based on facts the police didn't know or feel were important enough to include in their report.

Because police reports are not evidence the state does not have to prove all of the information or allegations contained in a report. Police reports are often full of errors, even when prepared by well-trained officers who are trying to be as accurate as possible. Not every detail contained in a police report must be proven in order for a domestic violence case to be prosecuted. But at the same time incorrect information can be used to show shortcomings in the police investigation, or that witnesses themselves gave inaccurate or inconsistent statements to law enforcement.

POLICE REPORTS ARE PUBLIC RECORDS

Police reports are considered public records. As such they are usually available from the police or sheriff's department within a few days after an arrest. There may be a small fee charged. The publicly available police report will not contain all of the witness statements, photographs, or other materials that can be provided through the discovery process.

The police report can be helpful in letting the defense know what information about an arrest the police thought was the most important, and also to explain exactly what the allegations were supporting an arrest. Because police reports may be available so quickly after an arrest, sometimes weeks or months sooner than the other discovery materials, obtaining the report can be an important first step in beginning a defense.

CHAPTER 14

GENERAL SESSIONS DOMESTIC VIOLENCE CHARGES DV 2ND DEGREE, DV 1ST DEGREE AND DVHAN

MANY DOMESTIC VIOLENCE CASES ARE BROUGHT IN WHAT IS CALLED the Court of General Sessions. This is court held in your county courthouse. There are three domestic violence charges that always go to General Sessions: DV 2nd Degree, DV 1st Degree and DVHAN. Any charge brought in General Sessions can result in serious prison time if you are convicted, so it is important that you begin working on your case right away if your case is pending there. You can be charged with DV 2nd or DV 3rd Degree on a traffic ticket. DV 1st Degree and DVHAN cases always require an arrest warrant.

DV 2ND DEGREE

The 2015 South Carolina Domestic Violence Reform Act turned many routine domestic violence cases into extremely serious DV 2nd Degree charges. This is a major misdemeanor charge that is prosecuted in the Court of General Sessions. All

DV 2nd charges can result in a possible sentence of up to three years in the South Carolina Department of Corrections.

There are a few ways that a domestic violence charge can be brought as a DV 2nd Degree instead of a DV 3rd Degree:

- If the defendant caused or attempted to cause moderate bodily harm to a household member; or
- If the defendant violated any protection order or restraining order from any court; or
- If the defendant has a prior domestic violence conviction within the past 10 years; or
- Children were in the vicinity of the alleged incident; or
- The alleged victim was pregnant; or
- The defendant was simultaneously robbing, burglarizing, kidnapping, or stealing something; or
- The defendant took the alleged victim's phone or otherwise prevented him or her from making a call for help; or
- There was evidence of attempted choking or smothering (i.e. – "he put his hands over my mouth after I bit him" or "she held me face down on the couch").

Only one of these factors involves the alleged victim being hurt. Moderate bodily injury is defined as:

> *Physical injury that involves prolonged loss of consciousness or that causes temporary or moderate disfigurement or temporary loss of the function of a bodily member or organ or injury that requires medical treatment when the treatment requires the use of regional or general anesthesia or injury that results in a fracture or dislocation. Moderate bodily injury does not include one-time treatment and subsequent observation of scratches, cuts,*

abrasions, bruises, burns, splinters, or any other minor injuries that do not ordinarily require extensive medical care.

DV 1ST DEGREE

DV 1st Degree is a felony prosecuted in the Court of General Sessions. It is punishable by up to ten years imprisonment in the South Carolina Department of Corrections. Cases are eligible to be prosecuted as a 1st Degree, rather than a 2nd or 3rd Degree when:

- The defendant caused or attempted to cause great bodily injury; or
- The defendant committed a DV 3rd Degree while using a firearm in any manner (no requirement to threaten with or point the gun); or
- When the defendant has two or more prior domestic violence convictions in the past ten years; or
- The defendant causes moderate bodily harm while:
    - ★ Violating a Protection Order; or
    - ★ Children are in the vicinity; or
    - ★ The alleged victim is pregnant; or
    - ★ The alleged victim was being chocked or smothered; or
    - ★ The defendant was simultaneously robbing, burglarizing, kidnapping or trying to steal something; or
    - ★ Taking the alleged victim's phone or otherwise preventing them from calling for help.

Great bodily injury is defined as:

Bodily injury which causes a substantial risk of death or which causes serious, permanent disfigurement or protracted loss or impairment of the function of a bodily member or organ.

When someone has a prior criminal record showing a conviction for domestic violence, he can then be charged with a DV 2nd Degree or DV 3rd Degree. For a prior case to count, it must have happened within the past ten years. Also, you had to be convicted. If your previous case was dismissed for any reason (plea bargain to a lower charge, pre-trial intervention or being found not guilty), then it will not affect your current case. Domestic violence convictions from another state can be used if that state's law is similar enough to South Carolina's.

DV 2nd Degree and DV 3rd Degree do not necessarily mean 2nd or 3rd offense. Anyone can be charged with these offenses without regard to their prior criminal record.

If you are in a new relationship, your domestic violence charges do not start over again. I have been asked before, "I've got a new wife now, does my DV count start over?" Unfortunately, it does not.

Help your lawyer verify your prior record to see if you really do have prior qualifying offense. Many times, people are charged when their previous charges are too old or were not convictions.

When someone has been arrested for DV 2nd Degree or DV 1st Degree, sometimes they are allowed to plead guilty to a lower-level offense as part of their plea bargain. For example, someone who has a DV 2nd Degree charge may be allowed to enter a guilty plea to DV 3rd Degree in order to avoid a lengthy prison or probationary sentence. Many plea bargains are accepted in Transfer Court, which is described in the next chapter.

KIDNAPPING

I am seeing more and more situations where the police are charging kidnapping along with a felony domestic violence charge. Kidnapping in South Carolina is a very serious crime. It carries a maximum sentence of up to thirty years in prison, and the court can even require sex offender registration. Kidnapping can technically occur by simply holding someone in place or blocking their exit from a room. There is no requirement that someone be held for an extended period of time or transported from one place to another.

DVHAN

DVHAN stands for Domestic Violence of a High and Aggravated Nature. This is the most serious domestic violence offense in South Carolina. It is a felony, prosecuted in the Court of General Sessions. It carries the highest possible penalty for any domestic violence crime, up to twenty years in prison.

For a domestic violence incident to qualify as a DVHAN, the same household member relationship required for other charges must exist. There is no requirement under the law that a physical injury occurred, but the incident must be "under circumstances manifesting extreme indifference to the value of human life." This has to be under circumstances that either made the alleged victim suffer "great bodily injury" or fear "great bodily injury or death."

The Domestic Violence Reform Act of 2015 made substantive changes to the DVHAN law. Although it doubled the maximum penalty, it specified that only the most serious allegations should qualify for this charge. As a result DVHAN is not being charged as frequently. Anyone charged with DVHAN should immediately take note that their case has been determined to be the "worst of the worst" and do everything they can to assist with their defense.

CHAPTER 15

GENERAL SESSIONS APPEARANCES

SOME DOMESTIC VIOLENCE CASES ARE ASSIGNED TO GENERAL Sessions Court. This court is located at the main county courthouse. General Sessions level include DV 2nd Degree, DV 1st Degree and DVHAN. In some counties DV 3rd charges are also brought in General Sessions.

An appearance in General Sessions is not a formal trial or a hearing in front of a judge. You will check in with your attorney and the prosecutor and then be given a date to return.

If your case is pending in General Sessions, you will be given the date and time of your first appearance. The initial appearance is not a real court or trial date, like it would be for a DV 3rd Degree. You will most likely not even see a judge in the courtroom. You should not try to talk to the prosecutor or anyone else about your case. Let your attorney do all of the talking.

Appearances are usually held in the largest courtroom available. It is not unusual for several hundred defendants to appear at the same time. Most are not charged with domestic violence but with other offenses such as drug trafficking, murder, or armed robbery. Sometimes, the courtroom becomes so crowded that family members or friends are told to wait outside. Typically, the alleged victim in your case or the police officer who arrested you will not be there.

At the appearance, your attorney will check in with the prosecutor assigned to your case. You will then be given a date and time to return, called a follow up appearance. In most counties, it is required that all defendants personally appear for their first appearance. Some counties may allow defendants to be excused as long as they have hired a lawyer. Unless your lawyer specifically tells you that you are excused, you need to be present. If you fail to appear, a bench warrant can be issued for your arrest.

ADVICE ON YOUR GENERAL SESSIONS APPEARANCE

- Be at the courthouse at least a few minutes early.
- Do not talk to anyone other than your lawyer.
- Wear appropriate clothes. No shorts or t-shirts. Do not use drugs or alcohol prior to going to your appearance.
- If you have a bail bondsman, be sure that you notify them that you went to your first appearance and let them know when you are supposed to return to court.
- Make sure when you leave you know the date you are supposed to return for a follow up appearance.
- If you also have magistrate or municipal court level companion charges, it is possible for you to have separate appearance dates for those charges. Be sure to keep up with all of your court dates.

CHAPTER 16

PRELIMINARY HEARINGS

THIS CHAPTER APPLIES TO CASES THAT ARE BEING REFERRED TO the Court of General Sessions. This includes DV 2nd Degree, DV 1st Degree and DVHAN cases. A preliminary hearing is a probable cause hearing presided over by a magistrate judge. Only cases that are referred to General Sessions are eligible for a preliminary hearing. To request a preliminary hearing, you must do so in writing within 10 days of Bond Court. Bond Court will provide a form for the defendant to sign. The request can also be submitted by your lawyer.

Preliminary hearings are usually scheduled within 30-90 days after the arrest, but it can be longer depending on the location of your case. In some counties, a prosecutor will represent the state; in other areas, the police will handle the hearing. At a preliminary hearing, the court will be concerned with whether or not a crime occurred and whether or not the person who was arrested is guilty. This hearing is not a comprehensive trial, nor does the court make a finding of "guilty" or "not guilty." It is simply a procedural hearing allowing the defendant an opportunity to question the prosecution about the alleged facts supporting an arrest.

The hearings are conducted one at a time, each usually lasting 5-10 minutes. In many cases, only one witness appears for the state and that witness may or may not have any first-hand knowledge about your case. That witness will tell the judge what the basis is for the defendant's arrest. Your lawyer can ask the witness questions (called cross examination). The defendant does not testify at the hearing. At the end of the hearing, the judge will either dismiss or modify the charge, or forward the case to General Sessions. Most cases are allowed to continue to General Sessions, even if the evidence against the defendant is very weak.

In many ways the judge's decision in a preliminary hearing is advisory only to the prosecutor. The prosecutor is still allowed to move forward with an indictment, which will allow the case to continue in General Sessions. Regardless, these hearings can still benefit the defense.

TIPS FOR PRELIMINARY HEARING SUCCESS

- Be sure to hire a lawyer before the scheduled preliminary hearing date. That way, the lawyer will be better prepared for the hearing than if he had been hired at the last minute.
- Do not be disappointed if the judge does not dismiss the case, even if it appears to be weak.
- Consider hiring a court reporter to make an official record of the hearing. Your lawyer will know how to hire a court reporter, but you will be responsible for the cost (usually $100-$200).
- If you hire a lawyer, you do not have to attend the preliminary hearing but going will help you understand more about your case and the legal issues involved.
- Preliminary hearings are not held in Magistrate or Municipal Court cases.

CHAPTER 17

TRANSFER COURT

MANY GENERAL SESSIONS DOMESTIC VIOLENCE CASES CAN BE resolved in a special term of court called Transfer Court. This is held in many larger counties in South Carolina. Transfer Court is presided over by a magistrate judge but is actually a term of General Sessions. The court can sentence someone to either a fine or a jail sentence. Probation cannot be given. Transfer Court is usually used only to process guilty pleas. Payment plans are usually offered for any fine or court cost imposed. Transfer Court can also be used to resolve cases that were either originally or have since been reduced to a misdemeanor offense, such as DV 3rd Degree or Assault and Battery 3rd Degree.

If your case has been referred to Transfer Court as part of a plea bargain, this is typically a good sign. Most counties that hold Transfer Court do so only once or twice a month. The docket will contain only misdemeanor cases. It is extremely rare for the prosecutor to be requesting jail time.

To achieve the best results, however, you must still take your court hearing seriously. Arrive on time. Dress to impress. Do not use drugs or alcohol the evening before court. This requires, at a minimum, long pants (or a full-length skirt for ladies), and a collared shirt that is tucked in. Be able to pay any required fine in full or be able to let the judge know exactly what type of payment plan you will need.

Because Transfer Court is used primarily to process guilty pleas, you should be sure that this is in your best interest. Many domestic violence cases are based on false or unfair allegations. Everyone who is charged with domestic violence should carefully consider all of their options, including fully contesting their case. But for many defendants, a Transfer Court plea offer is a successful conclusion to their case.

CHAPTER 18

PRE-TRIAL CONFERENCES "DO I HAVE TO BE THERE?"

AFTER A JURY TRIAL IS REQUESTED IN MOST MAGISTRATE OR Municipal courts, the next step in the process will be some type of pre-trial conference. Some courts call them by different names. In some courts, they are called pre-trial hearings or rosters. Pre-trial conferences are normally scheduled in all types of criminal cases, not just DV 3rd Degree. This chapter only applies to DV 3rd Degree cases. Pre-trial conferences as described herein are not conducted for General Sessions level charges such as DV 2nd Degree, DV 1st Degree or DVHAN. Because jury trials are expensive to conduct for the court and the police, pre-trial conferences are used to try to resolve cases before trial.

Your lawyer can advise you if you need to be at the pre-trial conference. There are situations where local judges and prosecutors may expect your attendance, when you are not legally required to attend. Your lawyer can advise you on the best procedure for your pre-trial conference. A pre-trial conference is not a trial date and not normally a date where the judge will discuss the specifics of your case. If either side has pending motions (such as a defense motion to lift the no contact order), it may be heard at the pre-trial conference. Otherwise, the judge may not be involved at all and it may simply be a meeting between the lawyers that takes place at the court building.

At the pre-trial conference, your lawyer and the prosecutor may discuss your case. Plea offers may be made. Examples would be changing a DV 3rd Degree to a "lesser" misdemeanor like public disorderly conduct or simple assault. They may also discuss pre-trial intervention (PTI).

If you agree to a plea bargain or to accept PTI, the court can finalize your case at the pre-trial conference. If your case isn't resolved and will go to trial, then a trial date can be set. You would then come back when the court is ready to begin selecting jurors for your case.

In many courts, the police are actively watching the parking lot looking for people who are violating a no contact order. They are looking for people arriving in the same car when a no contact order applies. Police also know that some people ride together and drop each other off a block before court, so they look out for one person driving up and then the other coming down the street on foot a few minutes later. If you are caught violating the bond restriction at the pre-trial conference, you can immediately be held in contempt of court and taken straight to jail for up to thirty days. The police or prosecutor may also directly ask the alleged victim if there has been any violation of the no-contact order. If the answer is in the affirmative, then you could face an immediate contempt hearing.

TIPS FOR PRE-TRIAL SUCCESS

Follow your lawyer's advice whether or not you should appear.

- Do not overly stress. It is not a trial date and you are not going to be questioned by the police or prosecutor about your side of the story.
- Dress appropriately. Do not bring a cell phone into the court building. Do not use drugs or alcohol prior to going to court.
- <u>Remember, your no contact bond restriction still applies.</u> Do not arrive with your partner. This is the fastest way to get held in contempt of court and go straight to jail. Do not sit next to, talk to or wave at your partner.
- Discuss with your lawyer the different options that may be available for you in advance. Be prepared to talk about PTI or plea offers. Also, be prepared to discuss scheduling conflicts you may have in the coming months in the event that your case is given a trial date.

CHAPTER 19

THE TRIAL OF THE DOMESTIC VIOLENCE CASE

This chapter discusses how a criminal trial in South Carolina is conducted. The information is applicable both to cases pending in General Sessions or in the Magistrate or Municipal Court.

1. One of the first steps in a trial is to select the jury. There will be six jurors in a Magistrate or Municipal Court case. There are twelve jurors in a General Sessions case. Neither the Defendant nor the State actually selects the jurors; instead the court will randomly select names and the defendant and the state each have a limited opportunity to exclude picked jurors from the case.

2. There may be pre-trial motions made by the prosecutor or the defense attorney. Pre-trial motions typically have to do with questions regarding certain types of evidence. For example, if the defense wants to exclude any reference to statements made before Miranda was provided, they could make that request as a pre-trial motion. Another common pre-trial motion is to sequester witnesses, which means to

make everyone (other than the main officer, the alleged victim, and the defendant), sit outside until it is their turn to testify.

3. Both the prosecutor and defense attorney will have an opportunity to give an opening statement. An opening statement is a chance for each side to introduce themselves to the jury and tell them what they evidence in the case will be.

4. After the opening statements the prosecutor will then get to present the State's case. This is the stage of the case were the police officer, alleged victim, and other witnesses the State has will be called to testify. The prosecutor will ask each witness questions, and then the defense attorney will have an opportunity to cross-examine each witness.

5. At the conclusion of the State's case the judge will normally stop the case in order to allow the defendant to make a motion for directed verdict. In a directed verdict motion the defendant is asking to dismiss the case as a legal matter. The judge is only allowed to considered whether or not any evidence exists that could support the charge, not the weight of the evidence. Most directed verdict motions are denied.

6. The defense will then be given an opportunity to call witnesses. The defense does not have to call any witnesses. If the defense does call any witnesses, including the defendant, the prosecutor will have the opportunity to cross-examine them.

7. After the conclusion of the Defendant's case the next step is closing arguments. These are presentations by the prosecutor

and the defense attorney to the jury about the case and what the evidence means.

8. The judge will then read a long list of instructions to the jury called jury charges. These are the instructions as to how the jury should conduct deliberations, and explanations as to the law that the court finds should apply in your case.

9. The jury will then begin deliberations. The jury's deliberation is conducted in secret. There is no time limit on how long the jury will take to decide any given case. Some cases are decided in only a few minutes. Other case may take several hours, or even more than one day to decide.

10. If the jury finds the defendant "not-guilty" the defendant's case will be over. The State cannot appeal. The defendant will not be sentenced, and will not have to go to jail or pay any court costs or fines.

11. If the jury finds the defendant "guilty" then the judge will decide sentencing. The judge will consider the exact charge, the Defendant's prior criminal record, and the specific circumstances of the offense in setting the sentence.

For many defendants, trial is the first opportunity they have to go to court and fully contested their charge. A trial, and specifically a trial by jury, is the most important protection that anyone has against false or unfair criminal charges. You should make sure that you are fully prepared for court, and that you have given your lawyer all of the information and evidence that he needs to best defend you.

When the jury decides your case they will be considering whether or not the State has proven you guilty beyond a reasonable doubt. All of the jurors must agree one way or the other in order to have a final verdict. If they jurors cannot all agree it is called a "hung jury." If the judge determines that you have a "hung jury" he will declare a mistrial. This means that your case wasn't resolved, and the State can bring you back later for another trial. There is no limit to how many times the State can try your case if the jury cannot ever reach a decision, but most of the time the prosecutor will stop after one or two tries.

I believe that everyone who is charged with any level of domestic violence should always consider taking their case to trial. Not every case can be favorably resolved through negotiations. And oftentimes the best plea bargains or sentence reductions are only made available to Defendants and\or defense attorneys who indicate a willingness to fully challenge their case.

TIPS FOR SUCCESS AT TRIAL

- Make sure you meet with your lawyer before your court date to review the case against you and what you will say if you decide to testify.
- If you have witnesses that you want to come to court to testify on your behalf let your lawyer know this as soon as possible. It isn't always possible to notify witnesses at the last minute.
- Dress for the occasion. You want to ensure that you are dressed appropriately to go in front of the jury. They are missing work or time with their family to hear your case. You need to show them that you take your case seriously and respect their time in order to get the best results.
- Do not use drugs or alcohol the day before your trial. I've seen many defendants try to "relax" the evening before trial,

only to appear hung over and lethargic in front of their jury. This is never helpful.

- Try to have enough money to pay a fine. Because it normally takes months or years for a case to be scheduled for a jury trial the judge will not always offer a payment plan. Try to have enough money to pay the maximum fine if required by the judge. If you can't raise that much, be sure to bring as much as you can. Regardless of how much money you have brought with you to court your lawyer will still be asking for you to be found not-guilty, or for any fine to be set as low as possible.

Even if you are sure that you want to go to trial you should still consider voluntarily participating in domestic abuse counseling. Doing so will not be used against you in court, so it does not hurt your case. Among other benefits, attending counseling can serve as "insurance" in the unfortunate event you are convicted at trial. Defendants who have voluntarily attended counseling are going to be must less likely to receive jail sentences or a maximum fine.

CHAPTER 20

COMMON DOMESTIC VIOLENCE DEFENSES

THIS CHAPTER DISCUSSES SOME OF THE MOST COMMON DEFENSES that defendants facing a domestic violence defense or their attorneys raise. I believe that including this information in this chapter is important for a couple of reasons. First, it is important for the defendant and the defense attorney to try to be on the same page when it comes to what defense will be presented or raised in court. A domestic violence defendant, especially one with no or only limited experience in legal matters, may not automatically know how to clearly articulate their case to their defense attorney.

Secondly, many individuals, especially those facing an arrest after false or unfair allegations, may assume that the prosecutor or judge is going to immediately see how their situation is special and unique and find them not guilty. The reality is that the defenses in your case have been raised by hundreds or thousands of defendants before them. Until the defenses are fully prepared for court, they are likely to be considered little more than excuses, and not taken seriously. The role of a defense attorney is to assist in fully preparing and presenting your defense so it has the best possible chance of being considered by the court.

Although every case is different, most defenses to a criminal domestic violence arrest are going to fall into one of the following categories:

THE ALLEGED VICTIM IS LYING ABOUT WHAT HAPPENED:

This is probably the most common defense raised. This is a defense based on the premises that the alleged victim has made up the story to the police. In order for this defense to be successful there needs to be a motive or explanation as to why the alleged victim is lying. Here are some examples:

- The alleged victim believes that the defendant has been cheating on them.
- The alleged victim is trying to break off the relationship.
- The alleged victim is trying to please their friends or family who have never liked the defendant.
- The alleged victim was simply so overcome with emotions during an argument that they made a false allegation in the heat of the moment.

SOMEONE ELSE DID IT:

This is a defense that is raised when the alleged victim has been injured, but the defendant asserts that someone else is responsible. An example is an argument involving three or more people, when someone other than the defendant hit the defendant. This can also be combined with the "lying" defense, in a scenario where the alleged victim's injuries are self-inflicted.

IT WAS AN ACCIDENT:

This defense is a suggestion that any physical injury sustained by the alleged victim was accidental. In order to be guilty of criminal domestic violence or assault the conduct must generally be intentional, so if a court finds that the conduct was in fact accidental then that can be the basis for a "not-guilty" verdict. Here are some examples of this defense:

- The defendant quickly opened a door, striking the alleged victim.
- The defendant threw an object and it bounced into the alleged victim
- The defendant was asleep, and struck the alleged victim during a dream
- The defendant was only using his hands for emphasis during a conversation, and didn't mean to hit the alleged victim

IT WASN'T REALLY CRIMINAL CONDUCT:

This is actually a very viable defense in many cases that don't involve actual injury and are to be tried in front of a jury. Under South Carolina law the police may arrest someone for conduct that does not otherwise seem criminal, domestic or violent. The premise is that whatever occurred was so far removed from what should be considered criminal conduct that a jury should find the defendant not guilty. Here are some examples:

- During an argument a wife pours out a bowl of cereal on her husband's head
- A woman slaps her boyfriend in the face after he called her an obscenity

IT WAS SELF-DEFENSE:

Self-defense can be raised as a defense to a criminal domestic violence or assault and battery charge. In a self-defense case the defendant is admitting/suggesting that their physical contact with the alleged victim was solely made to protect themselves or others from aggressive conduct.

IT'S THE ALLEGED VICTIM'S FAULT:

Some defenses are based on the special situation or misconduct of the alleged victim. Here are some examples:

- The alleged victim has a mental health condition and was acting erratically as a result
- The alleged victim was having a side effect from prescribed medications
- The alleged victim was drunk, or high on drugs during the incident
- The alleged victim was having an affair and was looking to get rid of me
- The alleged victim has a history of making false allegations. I'm the second, third, or forth one she's done this to.

THE POLICE BOTCHED MY CASE:

One of the most fundamental of all defenses in a criminal action is to challenge the sufficiency of the police investigation. Solid evidence of police error or shortcuts can be a very effective defense to raise, especially in front of a jury. Here are some of the most common issues raised:

- Miranda was not timely given.
- The police only talked to one person involved, and didn't even ask for the other side of the story.
- The police failed to take pictures of the scene or of the people involved.
- The police threatened or confused the alleged victim into providing an exaggerated or untrue statement.
- The police came into my home without permission or a warrant.
- The police officer knows me or the alleged victim from before, and intentionally set out to get me.
- The police report is full of errors and incorrect information (although the police report itself is not evidence in a domestic violence case, the police officer can be cross-examined regarding its content).

WHATEVER HAPPENED CAN'T BE PROVEN:

A very common theme of defense for any type of criminal charge, including domestic violence, is that the State cannot prove what happened. Because a defendant is presumed innocent until proven guilty beyond a reasonable doubt, the State has the full burden in court. In situations where important witnesses are unable or unwilling to come to court the prosecutor may simply not have enough evidence to pursue a case or win at trial. Examples include:

- When the police officer has retired or changed jobs.
- When the alleged victim is unwilling to court to court.

Keep in mind that if the defense is based on simple witness unavailability that the prosecutor can issue a subpoena to force the State's witnesses to come to court. In the event that the witness still refuses to appear, or refuses to testify in court, they can be held in contempt of court and punished by the judge. Magistrate and Municipal Courts in South Carolina generally only have the authority to issue subpoenas to residents of the same county. This does not stop any other witnesses from voluntarily appearing.

Determining what defense is most important, and the fully incorporating into the case both pre-trial and during trial is an important defense tactic. Frequently the defense is reduced to a simple "theme" that the defense lawyer will use throughout the case. It can be presented during the following stages:

- In discovery and other motions filed with the court.
- In questioning and interviewing witnesses pre-trial (both for the state and the defense).
- In pre-trial negotiations or discussions with the prosecutor.
- In voir dire questioning of the jury panel.
- In the opening statement.
- In the cross-examination of the government witnesses.
- In the questioning and testimony presented of defense witnesses.
- In closing arguments.
- In the requested jury instructions.

Your defense attorney can help determine how early on in the process to mention your defense. In some cases the defense is raised almost immediately. In other cases it isn't mentioned until well into the actual trial of the case. Defenses such as these, aren't something that your lawyer will type of and file with the court in advance of your trial. It is very likely that you don't get to "see" your defense in action until your court date.

LEGAL DEFENSES MUST BE CONSIDERED

In addition to the defenses previously reviewed, there are also potentially legal defenses to a criminal domestic violence charge.

As an example, the household member relationship can be established when a man and woman have a child in common. However, most DV 3rd cases are prosecuted in Magistrate or Municipal courts that do not have the legal authority to determine paternity. As a result, unless the prosecutor is able to bring a certified marriage certificate or family court order establishing paternity then they may not be able to proceed as a domestic violence case. This is simply one example of a possible legal defense; there are other strategies that your lawyer may review with you depending on the exact circumstances of your case.

Another example is when a case is brought as a DV 2nd Degree or DV 1st Degree based on a prior domestic violence conviction. In cases where the defendant did not have a lawyer in one of their prior cases the State may be unable to use that prior conviction to enhance the current case. This is a type of legal defense that will be investigated and raised if appropriate by your defense attorney.

ACCEPTANCE OF RESPONSIBILITY AS A DEFENSE

You should also know that you may not have to raise any defense, or cast any blame on your partner or the police in order to achieve a successful result in your case. Many defendants can best help themselves and their case by accepting responsibility for their circumstances and then voluntarily participating in counseling programs or otherwise trying to make amends. For example, many defendants are able to have their cases referred into pre-trial intervention (PTI) without the defense having to say anything negative about the alleged victim or the police. An advantage to having a lawyer assist you with your case is that your lawyer will not be emotionally involved. As a result your lawyer is in the best decision to help you determine if acceptance of responsibility is the best route for you to take.

CHAPTER 21

SPOUSAL PRIVILEGE AND DOMESTIC VIOLENCE IN SOUTH CAROLINA "WHAT IF MY WIFE JUST REFUSES TO TESTIFY AGAINST ME?"

A COMMON QUESTION WE ARE ASKED IS WHETHER SPOUSAL privilege would prevent one spouse from testifying against the other in a domestic violence trial. Generally defined, spousal privilege is a legal rule that prevents one spouse from being forced to testify against the other.

Spousal privilege is based on S.C. Code § 19-11-30. It provides that spouses cannot be forced to testify regarding communications. In the context of a domestic violence trial, the spousal privilege is "owned" by the spouse who is the alleged victim or other witness. This means that it can be waived at their discretion. Spousal privilege is different from other types of legal privilege such as lawyer-client privilege, which can only be waived by the client.

Spousal privilege only applies to those who are currently legally married. One requirement for a domestic violence charge is that a household member relationship exists between the defendant and the alleged victim. Household members include spouses, former spouses, those with children in common and those who are now cohabitating or have formerly cohabitated. This broad definition covers many relationships where spousal privilege would not be applicable.

A South Carolina domestic violence charge can be based on one of three different types of allegations:

- Unwanted touching was made.
- An attempt was made at unwanted touching.
- A threat was made that unwanted touching would occur.

Examples of unwanted touching include such things as snatching cell phones out of someone's hand, throwing objects, pushing, pulling or hitting. There is no requirement that the unwanted touching actually result in any physical harm.

South Carolina's spousal privilege applies only to communications between spouses. This covers conversations, e-mail, letters and text messages. Our statute does not extend to observations made by a spouse regarding physical acts or their knowledge of other events independent of communications with their spouse.

Because the privilege only applies to communications and not physical acts, it does not cover testimony regarding domestic violence allegations involving unwanted touching or attempted unwanted touching. It does, however, extend to communications involving a threat of unwanted touching. For example, hitting your spouse with a pillow or throwing the pillow but missing would both constitute potential instances of domestic violence for which the spousal privilege would not apply. But someone telling their spouse, "I'm going to hit you with a pillow" would be a communication and a court couldn't require a spouse to testify to that communication.

It is also normal for prosecutor to issue a subpoena to the alleged victim in a domestic violence case. This means that if the alleged victim does not show up in court, they could be arrested for violating the subpoena. If it is a Magistrate of Municipal court, the court can only issue legal subpoenas in their own county. Therefore, if the witness lives across the county line, even just a few miles from the court building, the court will not have jurisdiction over them. It is important that if there are any questions about whether or not someone legally has to appear in court, that they consult with their own attorney. Legal ethics rules restrict a lawyer from telling the other side's witnesses not to go to court, so there are some limitations on the advice your lawyer could give the witnesses in your case.

CHAPTER 22

POSSIBLE WAYS TO END A CASE

THERE ARE ONLY A LIMITED NUMBER OF WAYS THAT ANY criminal case can be resolved. Just like when you flip a coin and it is going to come up either "heads" or "tails," there are only a few options to resolve a domestic violence case. No matter what the facts of your case are or which lawyer you hire, your case will be resolved in one of the following ways. This list includes all possible outcomes of any criminal case:

Guilty Plea:	When you plead guilty, you are admitting that you are guilty. You are giving up your right to a trial or to challenge the case against you. You are also agreeing to accept the penalties that come with a conviction. Anyone charged with any level of domestic violence has a right to request a guilty plea.
Guilty Verdict:	If your case is taken to trial and the prosecutor convinces the court that you are guilty beyond a reasonable doubt, you will be found guilty. You will then be sentenced by the court. Defendants

are not supposed to be penalized by the court for taking their case to trial.

No Contest:	When you plead no contest, you are not admitting that you are guilty, but are agreeing that if the case was taken to trial it is likely that you would be found guilty. In all other ways, this is the same as a guilty plea. You are agreeing to accept the penalties that come with a conviction.
Nol Pros:	This is a Latin term that stands for "we shall no longer prosecute." It refers to a criminal case being dismissed or dropped by the state. Most domestic violence cases cannot be dismissed this way due to the no drop policy.
Not Guilty:	If your case is taken to trial and the prosecutor is unable to convince the court that you are guilty beyond a reasonable doubt, then you will be found not guilty. Your record will be expunged. You do not have to pay a fine or attend any classes.
Plea Bargain:	A plea bargain may result in you being allowed to enter a guilty or no contest plea to a lesser offense than domestic violence or may include an agreement that you will receive a lesser sentence.

PTI: Pre-trial intervention is a diversion program whereby certain criminal cases are removed from criminal court. If you complete all of the program requirements, your case will be dismissed and your record expunged. PTI is offered only for domestic violence charges in certain parts of South Carolina and is only available with the express consent of the prosecutor.

You should discuss all of the possible outcomes with your attorney early in your case. Know that your lawyer will only be able to give you the best idea of your chances for any of these results after they have time to review your discovery materials. No lawyer can ever promise or guarantee how your case will be resolved, especially not during the initial meeting when you are trying to decide if you should hire them.

PLEA BARGAIN CHEAT SHEET

The following are the regular reductions offered to defendants who choose to plea bargain their domestic violence case. PTI is not listed because it is not a plea, although it can be used to resolve many charges.

- DV 3rd Degree
    - An agreement that there would be no additional jail time or a minimum fine.
    - Changing the charge to public disorderly conduct.
    - Changing the charge to Assault 3rd (0-30 day penalty).

- DV 2nd Degree
    - Changing the charge to DV 3rd Degree.
    - Changing the charge to Assault 3rd (0-30 day penalty).
- DV 1st Degree
    - Changing the charge to DV 3rd Degree.
    - Changing the charge to DV 2nd Degree.
    - Changing the charge to Assault 2nd (0-3 year penalty).
    - Negotiated probation.
- DVHAN
    - Changing the charge to DV 3rd Degree
    - Changing the charge to DV 2nd Degree
    - Changing the charge to DV 1st Degree
    - Changing the charge to Assault 3rd (0-30 days).
    - Changing the charge to Assault 2nd (0-3 year penalty).
    - Changing the charge to Assault 1st (0-10 year penalty).
    - Negotiated probation

Plea bargaining is not appropriate for every case. Defendants who have been falsely or unfairly arrested should always consider fighting their case in court.

CHAPTER 23

PRE-TRIAL INTERVENTION "GUARANTEED DISMISSAL!"

There is a special program called pre-trial intervention (PTI) that in some counties may be an option in certain domestic violence cases. Pre-trial intervention is run by the solicitor's office. Although every county in South Carolina has a PTI program, not all offices will allow a domestic violence case into PTI. This is for political reasons, the equivalent of saying, "We're a zero-tolerance for domestic violence county." In the counties that allow PTI in a domestic violence case, PTI can even be used to resolve some General Sessions charges.

If you were arrested for another charge in addition to domestic violence, both cases can be referred to PTI at the same time.

PTI is not always offered by the police or prosecutor to everyone who qualifies. For this reason, it is important that if you think you are interested in PTI you should talk to a lawyer who can help you determine if PTI would be a good fit for you. This should be done before your first court date. You will still want to hire a lawyer for your case because in the event that you are not allowed into PTI, you need to take immediate action to protect your own interests so that you are not unfairly convicted. Also, a lawyer can help argue your request for PTI to give you the best chance of being accepted into the program.

In the counties where PTI is a possibility, it is something that most people with domestic violence charges who qualify should consider. PTI is called a diversion program and in order to participate, defendants do not have to plead guilty or be found guilty by a court. PTI is, therefore, for people who might be innocent or might be guilty.

PTI takes an agreement by the prosecutor or the arresting officer, plus the court, to approve the referral. Once the case has been referred to PTI, it does not come back up on the court docket for trial. Defendants whose case is referred to PTI who either change their mind about the program or who get removed from the program will have their case returned to court for trial. Since it is considered a diversion program, participation is ~~not~~ an admission of guilt and does not mean that someone is agreeing they did anything wrong.

To complete PTI, defendants are required to fulfill between 30 and 50 hours of community service either at a location referred to by the PTI office or selected by the defendant such as a church or community center. Defendants will be required to pass drug tests to show that they're not using marijuana or some other type of drug. Defendant will also be required to complete a 26 week domestic abuse course, going once a week. Counselling must be done on a week-to-week format at a center that has been previously approved by the government. Regular personal or family counseling will not count.

At most approved locations, a domestic abuse course will cost approximately $750 for the entire duration of counseling. PTI itself costs an additional $350, plus the cost of two drug tests (about $70). The total cost for everything will be a little under $1,200. This does not have to be paid all at once. Counselling is usually paid weekly. PTI will collect $100 during your first appointment and then $250 during the second appointment. There are no fines or other court costs paid.

Once PTI is completed, your charges will be dismissed and all publicly available records of your arrest will be removed. PTI will take approximately seven to nine months to complete.

> *Some individuals considering going into the military should talk to their recruiter before agreeing to PTI. Military branches pay attention to all domestic violence arrests and have access to records not normally public. Your defense attorney and recruiter may need to speak to each other to come up with the best strategy for your case.*

Completing PTI can guarantee the best possible outcome for your case. Because of this guarantee, many individuals may want to participate, even if they think the evidence against them is weak. No judge, police officer, prosecutor or defense attorney can ever be 100% sure what a jury will do with a particular case. Defendants always have some risk that they will be surprised by a guilty verdict they didn't expect if they take their case to trial. Going to PTI eliminates that risk.

To give an example how PTI was able to help John:

> *John was arrested for DV 3rd Degree after Mary's sister called the police. She reported that when she was talking to Mary, she overheard John in the background yelling and making*

threatening statements. John has a good job. If he is convicted, he will lose his job and his family's health insurance benefits. After talking to a lawyer, John learns that he has a good chance of winning his case if he fights it in court. At the same time, he will never know for sure what might happen in court and he cannot afford to be convicted. At the pre-trial conference, his lawyer negotiates a referral to a PTI program. John agrees to enroll and doesn't have to plead guilty or admit to any wrongdoing. After completing the program, his case is dismissed and the arrest is removed from his record. John is allowed to keep his job and his family's benefits.

In order to qualify for PTI, a defendant generally has to have never gone through PTI before. There may be some specific programs that allow for a second PTI, specifically for CDV cases. You should ask a lawyer who regularly defends people of domestic violence charges as even the court staff may not know about all of the programs available.

Defendants also must have a limited prior criminal record in order to go through PTI. The decision is made on a case-by-case basis by the PTI staff. Generally, one or two small misdemeanors will not prevent someone from going into PTI. Several other prior charges or a history of felony charges may make it less likely that someone will be accepted. If you apply to PTI but are rejected, you will only owe that office the first $100 payment.

ADVICE FOR PTI SUCCESS

- Talk to a lawyer before your first court date to help you decide if PTI is right for you.
- Retain a lawyer to go with you to court to request PTI. It is not made available for everyone who is legally eligible.

Bringing a lawyer with you will increase the chance that the prosecutor or police officer will allow you into PTI.

- If you decide that you do not want to finish PTI after starting the program, you can ask to have your case sent back to court for criminal prosecution.
- Once referred by the court, keep all your appointments with the PTI office. Do what they ask you to do as quickly as possible so you can finish the program successfully.
- Do not use drugs while in PTI. You will be tested.
- Keep in touch with your bondsman. Remember, you have to be out on bond to do PTI. (It's tough to do community service behind bars!)
- When you go for your first PTI appointment, bring the following: a pen, photo ID, proof of Social Security number, a money order for the application fee and a copy of your ticket or arrest warrant.

CHAPTER 24

DOMESTIC VIOLENCE COUNSELING PROGRAMS

THERE ARE SPECIALIZED DOMESTIC VIOLENCE COUNSELING programs now throughout South Carolina. Many individuals who are convicted of domestic violence are required to attend these programs as part of their sentence. These programs are also required for those who are attending PTI.

After the passage of the Domestic Violence Reform Act in 2015, counseling programs must now be approved by the Solicitor or Attorney General's office. There is a difference between fully qualified domestic violence counseling programs that will "count" for your case, and other types of counseling or treatment that will not.

Approved counseling programs will last for a minimum of 26 weeks (and many take slightly longer due to required initial "orientation" sessions). Standard "anger management" or programs offered by the military or other facilities frequently do not qualify. Prosecutors generally do not give any weight to participation or completion of online programs.

Most programs will be conducted in a group format, led by a group leader. Participants will take turns discussing challenges they have faced in their lives and in their relationships, and work on developing communication and coping strategies to help them avoid and de-escalate conflict. Although the sessions are not "privileged" like discussions with your attorney, participants and group leaders are asked not to share the discussions outside of the sessions.

Sessions will be held once a week. There is a strict attendance policy, and after missing just a few sessions participants will be removed from the program. For those who have been court ordered to attend, this can result in sanctions, up to and including jail. Those enrolled as part of PTI can be removed from PTI and have their cases returned to court for prosecution.

If prior to or during the program a determination is made that an individual needs substance abuse counseling, then this can be added as an additional program requirement.

I have found that in many cases, defendants voluntarily enrolling in domestic abuse counseling can be a huge benefit to their case. This is because voluntary attendance is looked upon very favorably by the prosecutor and the court. As a result, I frequently encourage my clients to enroll. Voluntary enrollment can help increase the chances of:

- Having no-contact bond restrictions removed.
- Being referred into PTI.
- Having charges reduced.
- Receiving a reduced sentence from the court.
- A voluntarily dismissal by the prosecutor (even with the "no drop" policy in place!).

In order to get the maximum benefit from the program, it is necessary for you to fully participate. It can be difficult to open up about your personal life, especially in front of strangers. But most people who fully participate find that they get a real benefit from the program. Fully participating will also enable the group leader to give a good recommendation about your performance to the prosecutor or the court, and not simply that you are going through the motions.

You do not have to have a violent temper to benefit either. I have had many clients who were not-guilty of domestic violence still chose to voluntarily enroll. Many have reported back to me that they learned about themselves and how to best conduct themselves in a relationship.

Many women are now arrested and prosecuted for domestic violence. Because of this, many of the counseling programs now offer women only sessions. These sessions focus on the same issues that affect men, but from a woman's perspective. Many women have found that having women only classes allows for more openness and a better exchange.

When you attend a domestic abuse counseling program, either voluntarily or by court order, you will be required to pay a program participation fee. These fees are due weekly, usually at the beginning of each session. Costs may range from $10-$30 per week depending on exactly what program you are attending. These fees are not fines or court costs, but instead only go to the program provider.

CHAPTER 25

DOMESTIC VIOLENCE APPEALS APPEALING A CONVICTION

ANYONE CONVICTED OF A DOMESTIC VIOLENCE OFFENSE HAS A right to appeal. Most appeals have to be filed within 10 days, although some cases in Magistrate Court or Municipal Court may have a shorter time limit. Convictions of DV 3rd Degree from Magistrate Court or Municipal Court are appealed to a single judge at the county courthouse. That judge will not be a magistrate and will have experience in conducting trials in criminal cases.

> *Consult with a lawyer right away if you would like to appeal your conviction.*

It is always recommended to retain an attorney to help with an appeal. Appellate Court rules are not always easy to understand and if not strictly followed, can result in an appeal being dismissed before the issues are decided. If you represented yourself at trial, if your original lawyer does not handle appeals or you don't want your first lawyer to continue with your case, you should immediately locate an attorney to help you with this process. If you miss the deadline to file an appeal, even by just a day, you may be permanently barred from appealing your case.

To file the appeal of a DV 3rd Degree conviction, you have to submit a document called Grounds of Appeal to the clerk of court at the county courthouse. Copies must be delivered to the original judge and the prosecutor. This document must specifically state the basis for the appeal. You have to be as thorough and precise as possible. Many times in order to appeal an issue require that you first would have had to make an objection to the issue during the trial and had the judge rule against you.

After the Grounds of Appeal is filed, your original judge will prepare an official response called the Return. This will serve as the official record from the court about what happened in your case.

You can file an appeal from a guilty plea. However, you have to show that the judge made some type of mistake in accepting your guilty plea. Simply changing your mind about how you want to handle your case or just not being happy with the judge's sentence may not be considered a very good reason. You should never go to court on a domestic violence or any other criminal charge in South Carolina expecting that an appeal will give you an automatic do-over.

Cases that are appealed from either General Sessions or cases that are appealed past the county courthouse stage will go to the Court of Appeals. South Carolina's Court of Appeals is located in Columbia. Most cases will be assigned to a three-judge panel who will review prepared briefs submitted by the state and defendant along with official records about the case. There may not be a hearing, but the panel always issues a written decision. It is important to know that an appeal to a single judge at the county courthouse after a Magistrate or Municipal court conviction usually can be resolved in about three months. Appeals made through the Court of Appeals may take up to two years.

To appeal from General Sessions, you must file a document called a Notice of Appeal with the Court of Appeals and then with the clerk of court for the county that handled the case. This has to be done within ten days after the trial. You do not have to specify which errors you are appealing like you would for a Magistrate or Municipal court conviction. You also have to order a transcript. Thirty days after you receive the transcript (or longer if you request an extension of time), you will submit a brief to the Court of Appeals in which you point out the errors you believe were made.

Once a decision is made on the appeal, either the state or the defendant can appeal again, if they wish. The highest level of appeal in South Carolina is to the South Carolina Supreme Court. People have a right to an appeal up through the level of the Court of Appeals. They also have a right to petition the Supreme Court through a process called a "writ of certiorari" for a further appeal. However, the State Supreme Court does not agree to hear every appeal and if they do not agree to hear the case, then the decision of the Court of Appeals becomes the final decision.

In an appeal, the court is generally not concerned whether or not somebody is guilty or not guilty. The court looks for errors or mistakes made by the trial judge. In most cases, they don't look at the sufficiency or the type of evidence that was presented in court, only at the legal decisions made by the judge. They're going to consider matters such as should the judge have granted or denied an objection, should the judge have granted or denied a direct verdict motion and what instructions (called "jury charges") did the judge give the jury at the end of the case. Whether or not a jury or judge should have convicted someone is typically not something that an appeal can resolve. An appeal, of course, can result in a reversal of the charge or the granting of a new trial.

POST-CONVICTION RELIEF (PCR)

There's another process that is separate from an appeal but can have the same result. This is called post-conviction relief (PCR). It is not always well known, but you can file for PCR for domestic violence convictions in Magistrate or Municipal court. You can even file for PCR in cases where you do not have a lawyer and are representing yourself. Most PCR applications are based on alleging that the lawyer representing the defendant was ineffective in some way.

Post-conviction relief is something that can be considered by anyone convicted of domestic violence, but generally I recommend that you do not file a PCR application until the appeal has been decided. You have one year from the date of a conviction to file for PCR. If you appeal, the time the case spends on appeal is not included in that one-year time frame.

Unlike appeals where there is not always a new hearing, most PCR cases can result in full hearings where the defendant is allowed to testify to a judge about how their legal case was handled.

CHAPTER 26

INTRODUCTION TO FAMILY COURT CASES THE FIRST 30 DAYS

ALTHOUGH THIS BOOK IS A GUIDE FOR THOSE INVOLVED IN domestic violence criminal cases, there is some overlap with Family Court cases that may be brought at the same time. In my practice, I have represented hundreds of people in different types of Family Court cases and I have seen people use our court system in both fair and unfair ways.

The first thirty days after a Family Court case is filed can be a busy time. Usually, there are two things that a defendant has to worry about. One is getting a legal answer filed with the court and a copy sent to their spouse's attorney. The other is a temporary hearing (sometimes called *pendente lite* hearing).

Temporary hearings are usually set just a few weeks after a Family Court case is filed. They are an opportunity for a Family Court judge to issue a decision that will control how the parties and their children will live until the case either reaches a final settlement or a full trial date. It may take years for any given case to get to trial.

Temporary hearings usually last only 10 or 15 minutes. The parties are not allowed to testify before the judge. The judge typically looks at prepared witness statements and a financial declaration form. Some counties even limit the number of pages of witness statements that the judge will read. The judge will then decide any unsettled issues such as possession of the house, custody of the children or the amount of child support.

You must also file an answer to the complaint if your spouse served you with divorce papers first. This is a formal response to the allegations made in the initial pleading (the complaint). If you do not get an answer filed in time, you could be held in default and not allowed to fully challenge your case later in court. The answer will be prepared by your Family Court lawyer in their office.

It is very important that people facing a Family Court case consult with a lawyer experienced in Family Court issues well before their court date and before their 30-day deadline expires.

FAMILY COURT ADVICE

- Hire a lawyer as soon as you can after getting served with papers.
- Provide your lawyer with copies of your paycheck stubs and other financial records like bank statements and credit card bills. You will need these to fill out the required financial declaration form.
- Work with a lawyer to draft your written statement to be presented in court. Also, help your lawyer identify others who might write a statement to help you.
- Do not wait until the last minute to get documents to your lawyer. Try your best to get them ready at least a week before

so he or she can review the documents and make enough copies.

- Be on time (at least 15 minutes early) for all Family Court dates. Dress like the hearing is important to you. Remember that your no contact bond restriction still applies, so do not talk to, wave at or sit next to your spouse.
- Do not give up on your case if you are not happy with the outcome of the temporary hearing. Legal cases are marathons, not sprints. The temporary hearing is only the first stage of the race.
- Many Family Court lawyers charge for their initial consultation due to the sheer number of people shopping around for a lawyer. Do not be put off by a request for a consultation fee; it is one way many experienced Family Court attorneys limit their time to people who are serious about their cases.

CHAPTER 27

ORDER OF PROTECTION HEARINGS "FAMILY COURT AMBUSH"

A COMMON COMPANION TO A DOMESTIC VIOLENCE ARREST IS a petition for an order of protection. This is a process that is initiated in Family Court by an alleged domestic violence victim against their spouse or someone with whom they have children. Unlike CDV charges, which are brought by the state, an order of protection is brought by an individual. The courthouse usually provides free forms to start this process, and in many counties, domestic violence charitable groups may provide free attorneys to those claiming to be victims. There are no free lawyers provided for the accused, however.

These are serious hearings. Always consult with a qualified attorney before you go to any Family Court hearing. Do not answer questions or make any statements unless your lawyer gives you permission.

When a petition for an order of protection is filed, it will be completed by the Family Court staff with a date and time of a hearing. At that hearing, a Family Court judge will listen to testimony about what happened and then make a decision. If the judge grants the order, it will be entered into a national police database. This way, law enforcement can run a driver's license or ID and know immediately if there is a restraining order against the person in question. The punishment for violating a restraining order can be up to one year in jail plus the possibility of a separate criminal conviction.

Family Court can also order possession of a marital home, spousal support or alimony, custody of children and child support. The decision of Family Court usually lasts for six months unless someone either brings a new family court case or moves for an extension.

If you go to the Family Court hearing and attempt to defend yourself, anything you say will be transcribed by the court reporter. Copies will be made available to the prosecutor in your underlying criminal case. Remember, anything you say can and may be used against you. I have seen situations where defendants have tried to defend themselves at Family Court hearings. They have unintentionally said things that ended up hurting their case.

The best thing anyone who has been served with a Family Court hearing notice is to immediately consult with an attorney experienced in those types of matters. Do not try to go to court without a lawyer. If your lawyer advises you to remain silent, and not to testify at the hearing you should follow that advice.

ORDER OF PROTECTION ENFORCEMENT

If an order of protection is issued it will, among other things, prohibit any contact with the alleged victim. This no contact order is different than a bond restriction in that it can be immediately enforced by the police. There is also a criminal law for violating an order of protection in addition to the enforcement powers of the Family Court.

You should make sure that you do not violate an order of protection, even if have you a good reason for contacting the other party or their invitation. If everyone is in agreement to lift or drop an order of protection this is usually a relatively straightforward process that can be accomplished with your partner's help in just a few days. I have seen many examples where people were enticed into having contact that violated the order of protection, only to later have those incidents reported as violations after the next fight or argument. I strongly encourage you to not allow for those sorts of opportunities.

> *If you do receive additional criminal charges or Family Court paperwork alleging an order of protection violation you need to immediately obtain the services of an attorney.*

CHAPTER 28

DOMESTIC VIOLENCE AND DIVORCE "GAMING THE SYSTEM"

One of the main reasons people make false or unfair domestic violence accusations against their spouse is to gain an advantage in a Family Court case. It's not unusual for people who have a custody case against each other to try to seek out opportunities to get the other person arrested. They think it gives them a shortcut to winning their case. Many lawyers who practice in Family Court have had the experience of a client happily calling to report getting their spouse arrested. In the next breath, they ask if they can immediately win full custody or an alimony award.

> *One defense strategy is to obtain copies of all Family Court documents filed by an "alleged victim" and then use them in court to show how the alleged victim is attempting to game the system against the defendant. This shows a jury is how far some "alleged victims" will go to lie about domestic violence.*

Mary is unhappy in her marriage to John. She has met with a divorce attorney she plans on hiring for her case. The weekend after Mary hired him, she falsely reported that John had assaulted her. John was arrested for domestic violence. Later, John's defense attorney was able to show that Mary had hired a lawyer and started on her Family Court case immediately prior to making the accusations. The jury then understood why Mary would lie and found John not guilty of domestic violence.

Some people also believe that they can obtain a divorce faster if they have their spouse arrested for domestic violence. In almost all cases, this is not true. While you can get a divorce on the grounds of physical abuse by your spouse, many circumstances that would constitute criminal domestic violence in South Carolina do not rise to the level that Family Court would consider physical cruelty.

For example, under state criminal law simply throwing a pillow or a set of car keys at your spouse or even dumping a bowl of spaghetti on them constitutes domestic violence. For purposes of divorce law, Family Court typically does not consider those acts to be physically harmful.

Another example would be an argument between a husband and wife. Suppose the wife angrily pushes her husband down on the couch. He is not injured. It is likely that this could be considered an act of criminal domestic violence for criminal law purposes, but not an incident of physical harm for Family Court purposes. If the wife slapped the husband across his face and gave him some red marks, that also may be domestic violence. It also could be considered physical harm for Family Court purposes, but it's likely not going to be enough to obtain a divorce on grounds of physical cruelty. Taking it several steps further, the wife stabbing or shooting her husband would almost always suffice as grounds for divorce.

Even though a year separation is not required for the court to grant a divorce on the grounds of physical cruelty, the case still has to be ready to go to court in order to get a divorce hearing. In many South Carolina counties, it is not unusual for a Family Court case to take one, two or even three years to get to a hearing. So even when the Family Court technically can grant a divorce, there isn't available space on the court calendar for newer cases. So many times, there is no advantage in real world cases.

CHAPTER 29

ASSAULT AND BATTERY

THIS CHAPTER DISCUSSES THE CRIMINAL CHARGE OF ASSAULT AND Battery (or just simply "Assault"). There is a significant amount of overlap in the area of relationship violence cases between the Domestic Violence charge and Assault charges. Many instances of alleged relationship or family incidents do not qualify for the specialized domestic violence law. This is because of the household member requirement for a South Carolina Domestic Violence charge. A household member relationship only exists between a man and woman who are or were married, have a child together, or who are or have cohabited.

Many situations involving alleged relationship violence, or simply other arguments involving dating partners or family members, do not involve legal household members. The following are examples of situations where an Assault charge would be made instead of Domestic Violence:

- Individuals who are "dating" but do not claim to have now or previously lived together or cohabitated.
- Intra-family conflict involving children, step-children, parents and siblings.
- Incidents involving strangers or others with only a loose association.

There are three degrees of Assault charges:

1. Assault and Battery 1st Degree

   S.C. Code § 16-3-600(C)(1)

   This is a felony prosecuted in General Sessions. The maximum penalty is up to ten years in prison.

2. Assault and Battery 2nd Degree

   S.C. Code § 16-3-600(C)(2)

   This is a misdemeanor prosecuted in General Sessions. The maximum penalty is up to three years in prison.

3. Assault and Battery 3rd Degree

   S.C. Code § 16-3-600(C)(1)

   This is a misdemeanor prosecuted in Magistrate or Municipal Court. The maximum penalty is up to 30 days in jail. This is the most common Assault charge, and it is sometimes also referred to as "Simple Assault."

There is also an offense called Assault and Battery of a High and Aggravated Nature that is a felony that carries up to twenty years in prison.

Many of the same initial case strategies that would apply to a domestic violence case also apply to an assault charge. This would include the right to request a jury trial and to file pre-trial discovery motions. Other parts of the case are not similar, such as the application of the domestic violence "no drop" policy.

Sometimes Assault cases involving allegations of more substantial relationship violence will be prosecuted by a regular Domestic Violence prosecutor. Because of this, there are occasions where it is appropriate to use Domestic Violence style negotiating strategies, including voluntary enrollment in drug, alcohol, or domestic violence counselling.

The court is also legally allowed to change a charge from Domestic Violence to Assault while the case is pending. Additionally, the court is allowed to find an individual guilty of Assault instead of Domestic Violence if it isn't satisfied that a household member relationship exists.

CHAPTER 30

CHILD ABUSE ALLEGATIONS

THIS CHAPTER DISCUSSES HOW PEOPLE CHARGED WITH DOMESTIC violence can also face investigation or additional charges for child abuse. I've already covered in previous chapters how just by having a child present during an alleged domestic violence incident will enhance the charges. But you can also be charged with separate charges if the police think the child was actually assaulted or otherwise involved in the incident.

Examples of typical situations where child abuse charges are brought with a domestic violence charge:

- A parent is holding an infant while allegedly being pushed or hit.
- Grabbing or pulling on a child during an argument (such as to take the child away from the other parent).
- An older child physically intervenes in an argument and ends up being pushed back or struck
- Angerly throwing an object during an argument that accidently hits a child

There are two main child abuse charges brought by police. Unlawful Conduct Toward a Child and Cruelty to Children. Both can have serious consequences for the accused. These are not "stand-alone" charges, where someone is charged with child abuse for intentional acts done to children. Instead, as the examples above show, these are situations where the alleged child abuse is only incidental to an alleged domestic violence incident.

UNLAWFUL CONDUCT TOWARD A CHILD

Unlawful Conduct Toward a Child is a felony, and is punishable by up to ten years in prison. It makes it illegal for someone who has custody or is in charge of a child to do anything to place the child's health or safety at unreasonable risk. This includes both physical or mental health risks.

This is a significantly more serious criminal charge than even 2nd degree domestic violence. Charges are prosecuted by the Solicitor's office in General Sessions court. Those convicted face a felony criminal record, and the possibility of a prison or probationary sentence.

CRUELTY TO CHILDREN

Cruelty to Children is based on S.C. Code § 63-5-80. It is a significantly reduced charge from felony Unlawful Conduct Toward a Child, but nonetheless is still serious. The law makes it illegal or a parent, guardian, or person in-charge of a child to ill-treat, deprive of sustenance or shelter, or inflict unnecessary pain or suffering a child. Charges can be prosecuted in Magistrate or Municipal Court, and there is a maximum penalty of up to thirty days in jail or a fine. The maximum fine amount is actually lower than Assault and Battery in the 3rd degree.

The factual allegations of a criminal child abuse charge are challenged in many of the same ways as a domestic violence charge. The defense needs to consider the following:

- What exactly do the police think happened that resulted in the charges?
- Are there any actual witnesses who will support that version?
- Does the child have any physical bruises, marks, or injuries? If so, are there any other possible explanations other than involvement in a domestic violence incident?
- What is the child's version of events? Are they lying, or have they been coached as to what to say?

It is also important to keep in mind that parents have a right to exercise reasonable corporal punishment in South Carolina. This means that under some circumstances a parents intentional striking of their child might still be considered lawful conduct.

Many times, police officers will "over charge" someone and include child abuse charges based on false or unfair allegations. Police officers may believe that by including other charges along with a domestic violence charge that it will make the prosecutors job easier and more likely that the defendant will simply plead guilty.

CHAPTER 31

FREQUENTLY ASKED QUESTIONS NOT ANSWERED ELSEWHERE

How long does it take for a case to be resolved?

Cases take different amounts of time depending on the court in which they are pending. The fastest way to resolve your case is by pleading guilty at the first court hearing. Any steps you take to challenge your case will add time to the process. Challenging your case may take 3 to 12 months, or longer.

Should I call the police about my case?

One of the worst decisions anyone charged with a serious crime can do is call the police officer who arrested them. You are significantly more likely to hurt your case than you are to help it. Anything you say to the police officer, even over the phone, can be used against you later in court. I would not recommend that anyone speak to the police unless specifically advised to by their defense attorney.

If I am convicted of domestic violence, will I lose my driver's license? Will my car insurance go up?

You will not face any type of driver's license suspension or revocation if you are convicted of domestic violence. Even though your DV 3rd Degree or DV 2nd Degree charge may be given to you on a traffic ticket, it does not carry any points and will also not raise your car insurance rates.

My wife and I have children together. How do we work together with the no contact order in place?

This is a very common problem. There really is no good answer and even the suggestions usually offered by police or court officials may still technically violate a no contact bond. The best thing you can do is speak to a lawyer as soon as possible about getting the restrictions lifted. I recommend that you use a trusted friend or family member to help with the children when they are visiting back and forth between you and your spouse. Do not be together in the same place or you could be held in contempt of court.

I am guilty. I feel ashamed of what I have done. Why should I get a lawyer? What can be done to help me?

Although I believe that more people are falsely or unfairly arrested for domestic violence than any other crime in South Carolina, I have represented many individuals (both men and woman) who are guilty of seriously abusing their partner.

The first thing you should do is to be completely honest with your lawyer. Everything you tell your lawyer is confidential and protected by the attorney-client privilege. Your lawyer cannot do his best job for you if you lie about or downplay what happened.

There are many ways I can help clients who admits to me that they are guilty without lying to the court or making their partner look bad. I frequently encourage clients to voluntarily enroll in alcohol, drug and/or domestic abuse counseling. Prosecutors may be willing to reduce charges when they see someone is trying to get help. I have also found that judges are very receptive to hearing what people have done on their own to try to solve their problems.

I was contacted by a Department of Social Services (DSS) caseworker after my wife's domestic violence arrest. What should I do?

Always take DSS very seriously. DSS caseworkers have the power to make your life and that of your entire family miserable for the next several years. The caseworkers also know this. You do not have to speak to DSS caseworkers or allow them into your home unless they have a court order. However, if you do not, the DSS may petition Family Court for an emergency order to put your children into a foster home or place them with other relatives. If you had any children present during the alleged incident, you should plan on at least a call from DSS. You should also make sure that your home is clean and safe in the event a caseworker shows up without advance notice. Always be very polite when you talk to any DSS employee. Do not volunteer extra information. If they believe that you or your spouse are having mental health, substance abuse or other family problems, they are likely going to require that you or your spouse be monitored by DSS for at least several months.

Your defense attorney should be able to recommend an attorney with experience with DSS cases in your area. As mentioned earlier, make sure any attorney you hire is capable and is someone you trust to handle your case.

I hired the wrong lawyer for my case. How do I fire them?

Before you decide to fire your lawyer, I encourage you to clearly discuss your concerns with them. I have met with many people who fired other lawyers, only to learn that the reason they were unhappy was a simple misunderstanding or confusion about the court process.

If you have decided that you must end the relationship, you should tell the lawyer or his office and then follow up in writing. The lawyer should prepare a copy of your file for you. Please give your lawyer at least ten days to make these copies. The court will have to approve your decision. Usually, this can be done without a hearing if you hire another lawyer right away. The lawyers will prepare a substitution of counsel form for you to sign. If you are planning to represent yourself, many courts will require a hearing before allowing you to fire your lawyer.

I did an Internet search for my name. I found that my arrest and my picture have been added to several "mug shot" websites. Should I pay to have my name removed? What can I do?

This is a very common problem. Criminal records in South Carolina, including arrest photographs, are considered public documents. They are given out to anyone who requests them, which now, unfortunately, include the mug shot-type websites. These websites are run for profit and are not affiliated with the courts. Many are based overseas. If you pay money to have your information removed from one website, it may just show up on multiple others since they think you will keep paying. Because of that, I do not recommend that you pay money to any of these sites.

There is not an easy solution. I advise my clients to develop new web content that will be reported by search engines for searches of your name rather than the mug shot-type sites. There are companies that will create good web content for you for a fee, or you can learn how to do it yourself. In one recent case, I recommended that a client legally change the spelling of his name because their earning capacity would be significantly jeopardized if their business customers learned of the arrest. Although this seems extreme (and it is), it is a quick and relatively inexpensive solution that may prove effective.

I am the alleged victim of a DV case. I don't like how the case is going. Can I be represented by a lawyer?

The South Carolina State Constitution contains an important provision that applies to everyone who is listed as a victim of an alleged crime. It is called the Victim's Bill of Rights and provides that you have important rights, including:

- The right to be treated fairly.
- The right to have access to information about the criminal prosecution of your case and to be notified about court dates and allowed to be present.
- The right to talk to the prosecutor and let them know your thoughts about the case.
- The right to talk to the judge at appropriate times about your case.

You also have an absolute legal right to hire any lawyer you choose and to have that lawyer represent you during the case. Because of possible conflict of interests between a defendant and an alleged victim, it is usually not a good idea for the same lawyer, or even same law firm, to represent both sides in a domestic violence case. Alleged victims do not qualify for free or no cost lawyers appointed by the court. If you do hire a lawyer to represent you he does not replace the prosecutor, and is not fully able to participate in a trial or court proceeding in the same way that the prosecutor or defense attorney is able to.

I have an old domestic violence conviction I'd like to have removed from my record. Is this possible?

DV 3rd Degree or CDV 1st convictions under the prior law that are at least five years old may be eligible to be removed from your record through a process called expungement. Expungement involves a specific application process. Some people apply for an expungement on their own and some people hire a lawyer to do it for them.

Not everyone who has an older domestic violence charge on their record qualifies for an expungement. In those cases, we recommend that people consider obtaining a pardon. In South Carolina, pardons are not granted by the governor, but instead by the South Carolina Department of Probation, Parole and Pardon Services. There is an application process and a hearing conducted in front of the board. It usually takes at least six months to get a decision. Having a pardon granted lets people know that you have been "forgiven" for your past criminal record. You can apply to have multiple criminal convictions, including felonies, pardoned from your record at the same time.

What will happen if I am in the military and am charged with domestic violence?

Anyone who is convicted of any domestic violence charge will be disqualified from serving in the military. This includes a conviction for Magistrate or Municipal court level DV 3rd

Degree, even if the penalty was reduced to only a small fine or a counseling program.

If you are in the military and are facing any domestic violence charge you should understand that your entire career is at stake. It doesn't matter if it is your first offense, or if you are close to being eligible for retirement.

All branches of the military are generally very good at supporting its service members who have been charged. You will likely be referred to counseling programs and your commanding officer or his designee will be tracking your progress. We strongly recommend that you participate in all the programs the military makes available to you.

Many police officers and prosecutors are sympathetic to the special issues facing military personnel, and often times they will be willing to work with your defense attorney to come up with a solution for your case that allows you to continue to serve. This may include reducing the charge through a plea bargain, pre-trial intervention (PTI), or some other creative solution.

I was charged with domestic violence even though my partner hit me first. Can I claim self-defense?

You can claim self-defense as part of any criminal domestic violence or assault and battery case. If there is any evidence that you could have been acting in self-defense the judge is required to instruct the jury as to the law of self-defense in the jury charges. If the jury finds that self-defense applies you will be found not-guilty.

You may also be able to file a motion seeking immunity if your actions were considered self-defense. This is under South

Carolina's "Protection of Persons and Property Act." If an immunity motion is granted this will result in the case being dismissed. Immunity motions in this context were recently authorized in the South Carolina Supreme Court case State v. Jones, 416 S.C. 283, 786 S.E.2d 132 (2016).

The police arrested both of us (both the man and woman) and charged us both with domestic violence. What should we do?

In this situation you are both going to want to hire separate lawyers to represent you. Due to the conflict of interest the same lawyer likely won't be able to represent both of you (but there can be exceptions). The law requires the police to make specific documentation as why they could not determine who the primary aggressor was. You may be eligible to have what is called a primary aggressor hearing to ask a judge to dismiss one of the cases. Otherwise, when the case was to go to trial your lawyer will argue to the jury that if the police and prosecutor couldn't tell who was primarily responsible there is insufficient evidence to find you guilty.

My girlfriend refuses to leave my house. There is a no-contact order and I can't go home. How do I make her leave?

This is a common problem, and unfortunately there is not an easy or fast solution. South Carolina law provides certain rights to holdover "guests" that will preclude you from forcing them from your home without a court order. You will need to go to the Magistrate Court and apply for an eviction. It may take several weeks (or more) for the eviction process to conclude. If your girlfriend is angry with you she may choose to damage, destroy, throw-away, give-away, or steal your personal property. For this reason the police may give you one chance to go home and pick up your personal items. Use this time to remove anything valuable, or irreplaceable. Your defense attorney should be able to help you with this process or refer you to a real estate attorney who can help.

I was charged with domestic violence after an incident with my boyfriend. There is a no-contact order in place. However, he is now stalking me. He calls all the time and has shown up at my job. What do I do?

The no-contact restrictions only apply to you, as the defendant. They do not prevent the alleged victim from trying to initiate contact with you. Of course, if you do allow the contact then you will be in violation of the order and face a contempt sanction. If you or your family is being harassed or stalked by the alleged victim the first step is to normally have your lawyer reach out to the prosecutor or victim's advocate and notify them of the problem to see if they can ask them to cut it out. If that isn't successful the next step would be to ask your lawyer to assist you in filing for a restraining order. This usually will involve reporting the harassment to the police first before a court case is filed.

My lawyer notified me that the prosecutor has made a plea offer. I feel frustrated, because I've told my lawyer I am "not guilty" and I want the case dismissed. What should I do?

Your lawyer is required to disclose to you any plea offers made by the prosecution. Just because your lawyer has to advise you of a plea offer doesn't necessarily mean that your lawyer is advising you to accept it. If after consulting with your lawyer you decide that any plea offer is not in your best interest, you can simply turn it down. Most of the time a prosecutor will make a plea offer before a case is set for trial.

GLOSSARY

Appeal: A process whereby someone convicted of CDV asks a higher court to review their case for legal errors or mistakes made by a judge.

Alleged Victim: A term is used in this book to describe who the police think that a CDV crime was committed against. I use the term "alleged" because using the word "victim" by itself implies that it is a fact that a wrong was committed against them and goes against the presumption of innocence everyone arrested for domestic violence has.

Arrest Warrant: A legal document signed by a judge that serves as formal notice of the charges against you and also allows law enforcement to place you under arrest.

Assault and Battery: The South Carolina law of illegal touching that may or may not result in injuries. There is no household member requirement as in a domestic violence case.

Bail Bondsman: A type of insurance agent who sells bonds to people trying to get out of jail.

Bench Trial: A court proceeding where a judge alone decides if a defendant is guilty or not guilty of CDV.

Bench Warrant: A type of arrest warrant issued by a judge usually after people fail to appear in court or comply with the terms of their sentence.

Bond Court: A court hearing held a short time after someone is arrested for a CDV offense. The judge will decide how much money a defendant or a bail bondsman must post with the court in order to allow the defendant to be released from jail. The bond court also may impose a no contact order.

CDV: Abbreviation for "criminal domestic violence."

Cohabitated: This term is not defined by South Carolina law as applied to criminal domestic violence charges. It is usually described in court as living together as husband and wife.

Contempt: When someone disobeys a court order. In CDV cases, the most common contempt situations are where a no contact order was violated. Contempt can be punished by extra jail time, a fine or community service.

Conviction: When a CDV case ends with the defendant being considered a criminal. Convictions occur when a defendant pleads guilty, pleads no contest or is found guilty by a judge or jury after a trial.

Defendant: A person who has been arrested for CDV.

Discovery: A process whereby the prosecution must turn over certain types of records and documents to a defendant to help them prepare their case. Discovery usually includes police reports, witness statements, statements made by the defendant and photographs taken by the police.

DSS: Abbreviation for the "Department of Social Services."This is a South Carolina state agency that investigates reports of abused or neglected children. They may be contacted by the police if there is a report of a CDV occurring in the presence of children.

DV 3rd Degree: A misdemeanor punishable by up to 90 days in jail.

DV 2nd Degree: A misdemeanor punishable by up to three years in prison.

DV 1st Degree: A felony punishable by up to ten years in prison.

DVHAN: Abbreviation for "domestic violence of a high and aggravated nature." This is a felony charge that is prosecuted in General Sessions. It is punishable with a maximum of twenty years imprisonment.

General Sessions: A type of court held in the main courthouse of every county in South Carolina. It is the court to which all DV 2nd degree, 3rd degree and DVHAN cases are assigned.

Grand Jury: A panel of eighteen citizens that hears a brief summary about pending General Sessions cases in a secret proceeding. If at least twelve of the eighteen panel members determine that probable cause exists, they will issue an indictment.

Great Bodily Injury: An injury which could cause death, or otherwise a serious, permanent disfigurement or loss of use of a bodily member or organ.

Household Member: A legal relationship that must exist between a domestic violence defendant and the alleged victim. Must be a man and a woman who are either now or formerly married, have children in common or who now or formally cohabited.

Indictment: A process whereby the grand jury decides there is probable cause that a domestic violence offense occurred. An indictment is required to be present or specifically waived by a defendant in order for a case in General Sessions to be tried or pled guilty to.

Jury Charges: The instructions given to a jury by the judge prior to the jury beginning to decide a case. A defense attorney can submit proposed instructions for the judge.

Jury Trial Request: A request submitted to the court asking to have a trial conducted by a jury rather than a judge only.

Jury Strike: A court date assigned to select jurors for a pending case.

Jurisdiction: Whether or not a particular court has authority over a given issue or over a specific person. Without jurisdiction, a court cannot legally act.

Moderate Bodily Injury: This is the standard necessary to be guilty of DV 2nd Degree. It is more than a a minor injury that does not ordinarily require extensive medical are.

Municipal Court: The court owned and operated by a city or town. Both the police and the judge are paid for by the same entity. Previously, these were known as police courts. They have jurisdiction over DV 3rd cases originating inside the city limits.

Motion: A formal request made by either the prosecution or the defense to a court. Can either be made in writing or verbally in open court.

No Contact Order: A restriction usually put in place as part of the Bond Court process against a CDV defendant having any contact with the alleged victim. This applies even if the alleged victim consents to or initiates the contact.

No Contest Plea: A type of guilty plea where the defendant does not admit they did anything wrong, but acknowledges that there is enough evidence against them they would likely be convicted if they had a trial. It is the same as a guilty plea in all other respects.

No Drop Policy: A rule that prevents police or prosecutors from dismissing a CDV case out of court or solely at the alleged victim's request.

Order of Protection: A special type of family court hearing where someone claiming to be a CDV victim asks for help from the court as well as a restraining order.

Post-Conviction Relief: A process by which a defendant who has been convicted attempts to challenge the case by alleging that there was a defect in the court process. The typical allegation is that the defense attorney was ineffective.

Preliminary Hearing: A hearing held for cases pending in General Sessions where a judge determines if there is enough evidence to allow a case to continue forward.

Pre-Trial Conference: A meeting held between the CDV prosecutor and defense attorney for cases pending in Summary Court.

Pre-Trial Intervention: A program available in some cases that can result in the charge being dismissed by the court after the defendant completes counseling, community service and other requirements.

Probable Cause: The amount of evidence necessary to arrest someone or to have a case called for trial. It means that it is more likely than not that a crime did occur and more likely than not that the defendant is the one who is guilty.

Reasonable Doubt: The legal burden that the state must overcome to convict someone after a trial. It has been defined as the type of doubt that would make a reasonable person hesitate before acting. This is the highest burden imposed on any type of legal case in South Carolina.

Roster Meeting: Another term for a pre-trial conference used by some municipal courts.

Search Warrant: A legal document signed by a judge to allow law enforcement to enter into a private home or business, or to otherwise gain access to a private area or private records.

Sentence: The punishment that a court imposes on someone convicted of a crime.

Solicitor: The term used to describe attorney prosecutors who work in the county courthouse prosecuting cases. Outside of South Carolina, they would be called district attorneys.

Summary Court: The term used to describe both Magistrate as well as Municipal courts in South Carolina.

Transfer Court:	General Sessions presided by a magistrate. Usually held in larger counties to accept plea agreements to reduced charges and\or reduced sentences. .
Victim's Advocate:	An employee of the police department or prosecutor's office. Their job is to talk with alleged victims and assist them with the court process or referrals to social service agencies.
Zero Tolerance Policy:	A rule put in place by many law enforcement officers in South Carolina. It instructs police that whenever they respond to an argument between a currently or formerly romantic couple they should always arrest one or both sides for criminal domestic violence if they find that the law was violated in any way.

ABOUT THE AUTHOR

James R. Snell, Jr., has been a criminal defense attorney since 2004. He is originally from Spartanburg, South Carolina. Mr. Snell has a master's degree from Harvard University and a law degree from the University of South Carolina. He has represented clients in a variety of legal matters, including civil and criminal cases and appeals. He has tried cases to verdict in all types of South Carolina courts such as Magistrate, Municipal, Family and General Sessions. Mr. Snell has argued before the South Carolina Court of Appeals and the South Carolina Supreme Court. He also has represented clients in criminal matters in federal court. He is a member of the South Carolina Association for Justice, the South Carolina Association of Criminal Defense Lawyers, the American Association for Justice and the National Association of Criminal Defense Lawyers. He is also a member of the National Trial Lawyers Association and has been recognized by SuperLawyers.

His offices are centrally located in Lexington and Columbia and accept domestic violence cases throughout South Carolina. He has helped people with cases pending in the Upstate, Midlands, Pee Dee and Lowcountry. He offers free in-office consultations to those who have been arrested for any domestic violence offense. To schedule your appointment, call his office directly at (803) 636-8826.

For more information about his practice, visit *www.cdvlawyer.com*.